Weekend Smokin

Hot Grilling Pit Boss Recipes for Hot Days and Fun Weekends

By

Sloane Pope

The trademarks used are without any consent, and the publication of the trademark is without permission or backing by the trademark owner. All trademarks and brands within this book are for clarifying purposes only and are owned by the owners themselves, not affiliated with this document.

TABLE OF CONTENTS

Introduction

A Brief of The Pit Boss Wood Pellet Grill

The Pit Boss Wood Pellet Grill is the most technologically advanced outdoor wood pellet grill. It has touch-pad digital temperature control, an LCD screen, and a meat probe. The Pit Boss Wood Pellet Grill can cook many types of meat, including burgers, hot dogs, chicken breasts, and chops, with its patented porcelain-coated cast-iron cooking grates. This grill can also smoke for the entree course of a meal. It comes with an attractive stand that makes it easy to move around the yard for backyard living while still retaining all of its beauty.

The Pit Boss Wood Pellet Grill can cook the meat just the way that you want it. It simmers and smokes the meat with incredible consistency. Its patented technology can accurately control the temperature inside the grill even if you are at a campsite outside in the middle of nowhere. There is a big storm outside. It also has a meat probe that lets you have a read-out on your meat to let you know when it comes out perfectly cooked with no dry spots.

The Pit Boss Wood Pellet Grill comes with a variety of grilling options. It can smoke, roast, bake, and barbecue. This is a great barbecue grill that allows you to do multiple things all at once so that you can cook a large meal for your family without spending too much time in the kitchen.

The Pit Boss Wood Pellet Grill has an easy cleaning system that makes it possible to be cleaned up quickly after use.

What is The Pit Boss Wood Pellet Grill?

The Pit Boss Wood Pellet Grill is a versatile and efficient barbecue grill that can cook various types of meat with control. It features a patented porcelain-coated oven that will give you consistent and even cooking, along with customized settings for your desired type of meat. It can also be used to smoke other foods such as steaks, roasts, seafood, and more. It also has a touch-pad digital temperature control that can show you the internal temperature of your rib meat or burger without you having to remove them from the grill.

The Pit Boss Wood Pellet Grill is a highly attractive unit that serves multiple purposes while retaining its traditional beauty. It has been made with durable materials and is designed to match the campout theme of woodlands even if you are on a huge tent site or cabins in the middle of nowhere. This grill is reliable, intelligent, and designed with technologically advanced features making it virtually maintenance-free for years at one time of use.

Specifications

The Pit Boss Wood Pellet Grill is has a stainless steel cooking grate and case, as well as a metal sensor. The digital temperature controls have an adjustable setting from 100 to 450 degrees Fahrenheit, so you can control the heat yourself every time you use it regardless of the weather outside. This helps to eliminate any of the guesswork associated with grilling meats.

How to Use Your Pit Boss Wood Pellet Grill?

The Pit Boss Wood Pellet Grill is easy to use. Just turn the temperature setting to the desired setting and press the power button once. You can adjust the type of meat that you want to grill using its touch-pad digital temperature control. This unit also has an auto-defrost function that automatically keeps your food at a safe serving temperature so that it lasts longer and is better for your health.

The Pit Boss Wood Pellet Grill is a versatile grill that can cook a variety of meats. It has a porcelain-coated cast iron cooking grate and case, as well as a metal sensor. The digital temperature controls have an adjustable setting from 100 to 450 degrees Fahrenheit, so you can control the heat yourself every time you use it regardless of the weather outside. This helps to eliminate any of the guesswork associated with grilling meats.

The Pit Boss Wood Pellet Grill is portable enough to take it with you on your camping trip or motorcycle adventure.

The Pit Boss Wood Pellet Grill has a gas-powered grill that helps get your meat up to a certain internal heating point, so it cooks quickly and evenly without burning or overcooking your favorite foods. It also has a revolutionary wood pellet grilling system known as a smoke box that can help to cook food on the inside and out at the same time. This grill has been designed with an attractive stand that makes it easy to move around the yard for outdoor living while retaining its beautiful appearance and design.

Insider Tips of The Pit Boss Wood Pellet Grill

The Pit Boss Wood Pellet Grill is an excellent barbecue grill for those who want to have fun while cooking their favorite kinds of meat. It is also perfect for people who want to have a quality and consistent barbecue experience without hassle with charcoal or propane tanks. The Pit Boss Wood Pellet Grill has an attractive design and easy installation that makes it perfect for any backyard or camping site. The wood pellet grills are very efficient and are designed to give you great results all at once. They provide a fully-equipped set of different features to help make the process of using them extremely easy.

The Pit Boss Wood Pellet Grill is a great barbecue grill that can cook foods in several different ways, such as grilling, smoking, baking, or barbecuing through its patented technology. This unit is also very easy to use and clean up after every use, so you don't have to do it too often. This barbecue grill is designed with attractive features that will help you to serve your guests in style.

Pros

The Pit Boss Wood Pellet Grill has a stainless steel cover. It can be easily moved around the yard because of its attractive stand. It has a gas-powered grill that can help it reach a high temperature for even cooking or grilling. The Pit Boss Wood Pellet Grill also has an intelligent touch-pad digital temperature control with an auto-defrost function that makes it perfect for any weather.

Cons

The Pit Boss Wood Pellet Grill has been made from durable materials, but it is not rust-proof, which means you should keep it covered when not used to protect it from rust and weather damage.

13 Tricks To Smoke Everything

Smoking is a pretty tricky process, so when you get it right, people might say something like "wow" or "mmmm." It's going to take some time and practice to master the art of smoking, but when you do, this is what you'll be doing with your Pit Boss Wood Pellet Grill & Smoker:

- Smoking beer can chicken

- Smoking salmon

- Smoking brisket

- Smoking lamb kabobs

 - Smoked pulled pork tacos

- Smoking prime rib roast

Wood pellet smokers are safer than traditional barbecues because they do not produce as much smoke; instead, they use heat for cooking food. Here are some tricks to help you:

1. Add dry wood chips to the charcoal basket on the grill.

2. Use a smoker box or wrap wet hickory chips in foil and place them on top of heated coals for indirect cooking or use a smoker dome instead of charcoal briquettes in the grill for smoking with direct heat to create smoke but no flame contact with meat.

3. Use two separate pans of hot charcoal for indirect and direct cooking.

4. Leave the hot charcoal in the grill and close the lid to add smoke flavor to grilled food.

5. Set up a low-temperature fire in a charcoal grill, add hickory wood chips to the coals and place food on top of the grate about 6 inches above the coals. Close lid and smoke for 3 hours at this low temperature before grilling directly over flames or move the meat to indirect heat while keeping it above hot coals. Grill indirectly over low heat for 1 hour 30 minutes, then cook indirectly over high heat till done.

6. Use wood chips to start the fire, add hot coals to the top of the charcoal grate, use a drip pan on it to remove ash for indirect cooking, or use a smoker box over the bottom tray of a charcoal grill for direct cooking without flames.

7. Lightly coat food with oil before grilling and smoke it in the grill at 400°F (205°C) until the food is cooked thoroughly.

8. Let food rest for 10 minutes after grilling before consuming for best flavor, flavor retention, and texture. Take off most barbecue sauce on grilled meat when serving and save for pouring on the plate.

9. Use a chimney starter.

10. Use sealed foil packets for indirect grilling or a smoker box with a peaked lid to trap heat and smoke flavor in the food. Position food above the smoke, cover it with foil, and seal the top of the packet tightly if using a charcoal grill or smoker box with a peaked lid to control heat, flavor, and moisture in food open grills and flame for cooking.

11. Smoke wood chips until they are completely dry, and do not release any more flavors into the charcoal when you light it again.

12. Use a smoker with a water pan for indirect grilling and limit the temperature inside the grill so that food does not burn.

13. Add dry wood chips to the charcoal basket on the grill for indirect heat cooking or wrap wet hickory chips in foil and place them on top of heated coals for indirect

cooking or use a smoker dome instead of charcoal briquettes in the grill for smoking with direct heat to create smoke but no flame contact with meat.

Beef, Lamb & Pork Recipes

1. Grilled Filet Mignon

Servings: 3

Calories: 229

Cooking Time: 20 minutes

Ingredients:

- Salt

- Pepper

- Filet mignon - 3

Directions:

1. Preheat your grill to 450 degrees.

2. Season the steak with a good amount of salt and pepper to enhance its flavor.

3. Place on the grill and flip after 5 minutes.

4. Grill both sides for 5 minutes each.

5. Take it out when it looks cooked, and serve with your favorite side dish.

Nutrition: Carbohydrates: 0 g; Protein: 23 g; Fat: 15 g; Sodium: 240 mg; Cholesterol: 82 mg

2. Kalbi Beef Ribs

Servings: 6

Calories: 355

Cooking Time: 23 minutes

Ingredients:

- Thinly sliced beef ribs - 2 ½ lbs

- Soy sauce - ½ cup

- Brown sugar - ½ cup

- Rice wine or mirin - ⅛ cup

- Minced garlic - 2 tbsp

- Sesame oil - 1 tbsp

- Grated onion - ⅛ cup

Directions:

1. In a medium-sized bowl, mix the mirin, soy sauce, sesame oil, brown sugar, garlic, and grated onion.

2. Add the ribs to the bowl to marinate and cover it properly with cling wrap. Put it in the refrigerator for up to 6 hours.

3. Once you remove the marinated ribs from the refrigerator, immediately put them on the grill. Close the grill quickly, so no heat is lost. Also, make sure the grill is preheated well before you place the ribs on it.

4. Cook on one side for 4 minutes and then flip it. Cook the other side for 4 minutes.

5. Pull it out once it looks fully cooked. Serve it with rice or any other side dish

Nutrition: Carbohydrates: 22 g; Protein: 28 g; Fat: 6 g; Sodium: 1213 mg;

Cholesterol: 81 mg

3. Homemade Meatballs

Servings: 12

Calories: 453

Cooking Time: 1 hour 20 minutes

Ingredients:

- Ground beef - 2 lbs

- White bread - 2 slices

- Whole milk - ½ cup

- Salt - 1 tbsp

- Onion powder - ½ tbsp

- Italian seasoning - 2 tbsp

- Ground black pepper- ¼ tbsp

- Minced garlic - ½ tbsp

Directions:

1. Combine the whole milk, white bread, minced garlic, onion powder, Italian seasoning, and black pepper.

2. Add the ground beef and mix well.

3. Preheat your wood pellet grill on the 'smoke' option and leave the lid open for 4-5 minutes.

4. Line a baking sheet and start placing small balls on the sheet.

5. Smoke for 35 minutes and then flip the balls.

6. Let it stay for 35 more minutes.

7. Once it turns golden brown, serve hot!

Nutrition: Carbohydrates: 7 g; Protein: 42 g; Fat: 27 g; Sodium: 550 mg;

Cholesterol: 137 mg

4. Rib Roast

Servings: 8

Calories: 721

Cooking Time: 2 hours 10 minutes

Ingredients:

- Boneless rib roast - 5 lbs

- Beef broth - 2 cups

- Celery - ½ chopped

- Carrots - ½ cup chopped

- Rosemary - 1 tbsp

- Onion - ½ cup

- Granulated garlic - 1 tbsp

- Onion powder - 1 ½ tbsp

- Kosher salt - 4 tbsp

- Black ground pepper - 1 tbsp

Directions:

- Preheat your wood pellet grill to 250 degrees.

- Take the beef out of the refrigerator at least 1 hour before cooking.

- Mix the pepper, salt, rosemary, onion powder, and garlic in a bowl.

- Coat the rib roast with this mix. Set the roast aside after coating it well.

- Mix the onions, celery, and carrots in a high-sided pan.

- Place the coated roast rib on top of the vegetables. Place it on the preheated grill.

- After 1 hour, pour the beef broth on the container.

- Cook until the temperature reaches 120 degrees.

- Pull out the roast and let it sit for 20 minutes.

- Skim off the fat and strain the juice from the bottom.

Nutrition: Carbohydrates: 3 g; Protein: 42 g; Fat: 60 g; Sodium: 2450 mg; Cholesterol: 207 mg

5. Grilled Hanger Steak

Servings: 6

Calories: 133

Cooking Time: 50 minutes

Ingredients:

- Hanger Steak - 1

- Salt

- Pepper

- For Bourbon Sauce

- Bourbon whiskey - ⅛ cup

- Honey - ⅛ cup

- Sriracha - 1 tbsp

- Garlic - ½ tbsp

- Salt - ¼ tbsp

Directions:

- Preheat the grill to 225 degrees.

- Use pepper and salt to season the steak liberally.

- Place the steak on the grill and close the lid.

- Let it cook until the temperature goes down to the finish.

- Take an iron skillet and place it on the stove.

- Add some butter to the pan and place the steak on it.

- Cook on both sides for 2 minutes each.

- Remove the steak from the stove.

- Add the bourbon sauce ingredients to the pan.

- Cook and whisk for 3-4 minutes. Pour it over your steak.

- Serve with your favorite side dish, or have it with the bourbon sauce.

Nutrition: Carbohydrates: 6 g; Protein: 10 g; Fat: 7 g; Sodium: 180 mg;

Cholesterol: 36 mg

6. Smoked Peppered Beef Tenderloin

Servings: 4-6

Calories: 70

Cooking Time: 105 minutes

Ingredients:

- Cloves of minced garlic - 2

- Snake River trimmed beef tenderloin roast - 1

- Strong cold coffee or bourbon - 2 tbsp

- Dijon mustard - ½ cup

- Coarsely ground green and black peppercorns

- Jacobsen salt

Directions:

1. Lay the tenderloin gently on a large piece of clear plastic wrap.

2. Combine the garlic, bourbon, and mustard in a small bowl. Slather the mixture over the tenderloin evenly. Let it sit for an hour at room temperature.

3. Unwrap the plastic wrap. Season the tenderloin with the ground green and black peppercorns and salt generously on all sides.

4. Once it is ready to cook, preheat the pellet grill to 180 degrees for 15 minutes with the lid closed.

5. Arrange the tenderloin on the grill grate directly and smoke it for about 1 hour.

6. Increase the temperature of the grill to around 400 degrees. Roast the tenderloin properly for 20-30 minutes until the internal temperature of the

meat reaches 130 degrees. The time depends on the overall thickness of the tenderloin. Be careful not to overcook the meat!

7. Let it rest for around 10 minutes before slicing it. Enjoy!

Nutrition: Carbohydrates: 3 g; Protein: 10 g; Fat: 1 g; Sodium: 590 mg;

Cholesterol: 20 mg

7. Spicy Grilled Beef Steak

Servings: 6

Calories: 634

Cooking Time: about 1 hour and 22 minutes

Ingredients:

- Chili powder—2 tbsps.

- Beef rib eye—4 steaks

- Brown sugar—1 tsp.

- Worcestershire sauce — 2 tbsps.

- Garlic cloves — 2, minced

- Ground cumin — 1 tsp.

- Olive oil — 2 tbsps.

- Salt — 1 tsp.

Directions:

1. Mix salt and mashed garlic in a small mixing bowl. Add Worcestershire sauce, chili powder, brown sugar, olive oil, and cumin.

2. Use this mixture to coat the steaks.

3. Put the coated steaks and the rest of the rub in a large zip-seal bag. Let it marinate in the refrigerator for about 5–24 hours.

4. Prepare your Wood Pellet Smoker-Grill by preheating it to about 225°F. Close the top lid and leave for 12–18 minutes.

5. Smoke the steaks for about 50–60 minutes. Then, remove.

6. Increase the temperature to about 350°F and cook the steaks again to get an internal temperature of about 135°F.

7. Remove and allow the meat to cool.

8. Your dish is ready to be served.

Nutrition: Carbohydrate 34 g; Protein 67 g; Fat 13 g; Sodium 786 mg;

Cholesterol 160 mg

8. Wood Pellet Smoked Meat Loaf

Preparation Time: 10 Minutes

Cooking time: 60 Minutes

Servings: 8

Ingredients:

- One and ½ lbs of ground beef

- ½ lb of sausage

- ½ Cup of bread crumbs

- ¾ Cup of plain yogurt

- ¼ Cup of milk

- Two large eggs

- 2 Teaspoons of chopped garlic

- ½ Cup of Parmesan cheese

- 1 Tablespoon of dried parsley

- One teaspoon of dried oregano

- One and ½ teaspoons of kosher salt

- Your favorite BBQ rub 1

- Pinch of black pepper

Directions:

- Start your pellet smoker grill and turn it to a temperature of about 350°F to heat it.

- In a medium-sized bowl, mix all your wet ingredients; then, place the seasonings in it, mix the sausage and the ground beef altogether in a bowl, form a loaf of your mixture, then roll it into your favorite rub. Place the beef loaf on the pellet grill rack, then put the meat probe right into the center.

- Smoke the Meatloaf on High smoke for about 30 minutes at a temperature of 350°F until the internal temperature displays 160° F; it may take an hour

- Slice your meatloaf, then serve and enjoy its delicious taste.

Nutrition: Calories: 343, Fat: 25.6g, Carbohydrates: 10g, Protein: 17.2g, Dietary Fiber 0.5 g

9. Wood Pellet Corned Beef with Cabbage

Preparation Time: 10 Minutes

Cooking time: 30 Minutes

Servings: 4

Ingredients:

- A cut of corned beef
- 2 cups of water
- 5 to 6 red potatoes
- One head of cabbage
- Three teaspoons of garlic salt
- One teaspoon of ground black pepper
- 3 to 4 tablespoons of whole grain mustard
- 3 Tablespoons of melted butter

Directions:

- Start by rinsing the two sides of the corned beef under cold water for about 2 minutes to excess any excess salt

- Coat both the sides of the corned beef with two tablespoons of mustard

- Add the water and the corned beef to an aluminum pan and smoke it at a temperature of about 220° F

- Remove the stem and remove the core of the cabbage; then quarter it

- Melt the butter; then stir in about one tablespoon of mustard and about one teaspoon of garlic salt

- Place the cabbage quarters into the aluminum pan in each of the corners and core it side up so that it looks like bowls

- Chop the potatoes in half and season it with about two teaspoons of garlic salt and about ½ teaspoon of pepper.

- Place the potatoes along the edges of the aluminum pan between the quarters of the cabbage

- Cover with the aluminum foil; then turn up your wood pellet grill to about 280°F and cook for about two additional hours until the internal temperature of the meat reaches about 200 to 205° F

- Remove the aluminum foil and cook for about 15 minutes. Slice the meat, then serve and enjoy it!

Nutrition: Calories: 213.5, Fat: 15g, Carbohydrates: 8g, Protein: 7.9g, Dietary Fiber: 1.2g

Ingredients:

- Ten medium jalapeño peppers
- 8 ounces regular cream cheese at room temperature ¾ cup shredded Monterey Jack and cheddar
- cheese blend (optional) 1 teaspoon smoked paprika
- One teaspoon garlic powder
- ½ teaspoon cayenne pepper
- ½ teaspoon red pepper flakes (optional)
- 20 Little Smokies sausages
- Ten thinly sliced bacon strips, cut in half

Instructions:

- Put your foodservice gloves on if using. Wash and slice the jalapeño peppers lengthwise. Using a spoon or paring knife, carefully remove the seeds and veins and discard them. Place the jalapeños on a vegetable grilling tray and set aside.
- In a small bowl, mix the cream cheese, shredded cheese, if using, paprika, garlic powder, cayenne pepper, and red pepper flakes, if using, until fully incorporated.

- Fill the hollowed jalapeño pepper halves with the cream cheese mixture. Wrap half a slice of thin bacon around each jalapeño pepper half.
- Use a toothpick to secure the bacon to the sausage, making sure not to pierce the pepper. Place the ABTs on a grilling tray or pan.
- Configure your wood pellet smoker-grill for indirect cooking and preheat to 250°F using hickory pellets or a blend.
- Smoke the jalapeño peppers at 250°F for approximately 1½ to 2 hours until the bacon is cooked and crispy.

11. Garlic Parmesan Wedges

Ingredients:

- Three large russet potatoes
- ¼ cup extra-virgin olive oil
- 1½ teaspoons salt
- ¾ teaspoon black pepper
- Two teaspoons garlic powder
- ¾ cup grated Parmesan cheese
- Three tablespoons chopped fresh cilantro or flat-leaf parsley (optional)
- ½ cup blue cheese or ranch dressing per serving, for dipping (optional)

Instructions:

- Gently scrub the potatoes with cold water using a vegetable brush and allow the potatoes to dry.
- Cut the potatoes lengthwise in half, then cut those halves into thirds.
- Use a paper towel to wipe away all the moisture that is released when you cut the potatoes. Moisture prevents the wedges from getting crispy.
- Place the potato wedges, olive oil, salt, pepper, and garlic powder in a large bowl, toss lightly with your hands, and make sure the oil and spices are distributed evenly.
- Arrange the wedges in a single layer on a nonstick grilling tray/pan/basket (about 15 × 12 inches).
- Configure your wood pellet smoker-grill for indirect cooking and preheat to 425°F using any type of wood pellets.
- Place the grilling tray in your preheated smoker grill and roast the potato wedges for 15 minutes before turning. Roast the potato wedges for an additional 15 to 20 minutes until potatoes are fork-tender on the inside and crispy golden brown on the outside.
- Sprinkle the potato wedges with Parmesan cheese and garnish with cilantro or parsley, if desired. Serve with blue cheese or ranch dressing for dipping, if desired.

12. Traeger Smoked Jalapeno Poppers

Ingredients:

- 12 jalapeño peppers
- 8-ounces cream cheese, room temperature
- Ten pieces of bacon

Instructions:

- Preheat your Traeger or another wood-pellet grill to 350°.
- Wash and cut the tops off of the peppers, and then slice them half the long way. Scrape the seeds and the membranes out, and set them aside.
- Spoon softened cream cheese into the popper, and wrap with bacon and secure with a toothpick.
- Place on wire racks that are non-stick or sprayed with non-stick spray, grill for 20-25 minutes, or until the bacon is cooked.

13. Double Smoked Ham on Pellet Grill

Ingredients:

- One pre-cook cured smoked ham
- 2 liters of Pepsi, Coke, or Dr. Pepper

Instructions:

- Start by preheating your grill to 500 degrees.
- Place your ham long side down on the grill for 10 -20 minutes. You want to sear the ham on all sides of the outside. So, rotate the ham around and build a nice sear all around.
- Once your ham is fully seared, place in a pan and pour some pop over the ham. This is what you will use for basting throughout the cooking process.
- Drop the heat down to 225 degrees and baste your ham every 20-30 minutes for 4 hours.
- Once the 4 hours is up, pull the ham from the grill, and slice and serve.

14. Reverse Seared NY Strip Steak

Ingredients:

- 4 (1-1/2" Inch Thick) New York Strip Steaks
- Traeger Beef Rub
- 4 Tbsp Butter

Instructions:

- When ready to cook, set the Traeger to 225°F and preheat, lid closed for 15 minutes. For optimal flavor, use Super Smoke if available.
- While the grill is coming up to temperature, season the steaks with Traeger Beef rub.
- Place the steaks in the grill and smoke for 60 minutes or until they reach an internal temperature of 105 to 110°F. Remove steaks from the grill and set them on the counter to rest.
- Increase the grill temperature to 450°F. For optimal results, set to 500°F if available and let it come up to temperature with the lid close, about 10 minutes.
- Return steaks to grill and sear for 4 minutes. Flip steaks and add 1 tbsp butter to each steak.

- Sear for another 4 minutes and check the internal temperature. The desired finish temperature is 130 to 135°F for medium-rare.
- Once the desired temperature is reached, remove steaks from the grill. Let rest 5 minutes. Enjoy!

15. Smoked Beef Fillets

Preparation Time: 20m

Cooking Time: 3 hours

Serving: 8

Ingredients:

- 4 lbs. beef fillets
- 1 tbsp. oregano, dried
- 2 tbsps. Olive oil
- Four minced garlic cloves
- ½ tbsp. Salt
- ½ tbsp. black pepper, ground

Directions:

1. Preheat smoker to 225F. Use cherry or mesquite wood.
2. Season the meat with oregano, salt, garlic, and pepper.
3. Heat some oil in a large pan and quickly sear the meat on both sides, 1-2 minutes per side.
4. Wrap each fillet in aluminum foil, leaving the open top.
5. Drizzle the beef with olive oil and place it into the smoker.
6. Smoke the beef for 1 ½ hour for medium-rare or 2 ½ hours for well done.
7. Serve after.

Nutrition: Calories: 321 Total Carbohydrate 15.5g 6% Dietary Fiber: 0.3g 1% Total Sugars 13.5g Protein: 42.2g Vitamin D: 0mcg 0% Calcium: 25mg 2% Iron: 4mg 24% Potassium: 454mg 10%

16. Smoked Beef Stew

Preparation Time: 20m

Cooking Time: 2 hours

Serving: 5

Ingredients:

- lbs. stew beef, cubed

- 2 carrots
- 4 potatoes
- ¼ onion
- 1 clove garlic

- 2 tsps. Pepper
- 2½ tsp. salt
- 2 tsps. Thyme, dried

Directions:

1. Put the vegetables and the seasoning ingredients in a pot and put the pot on the smoker. The vegetables should begin to cook before adding the beef to gain the smoky texture and add flavor to the meal.
2. Apply pepper and salt to the beef cubes and smoke them individually for at least one to two hours. After that, you can mix the beef with the content of the first pot and start smoking the whole lot for a couple more hours.

Nutrition: Calories: 334 Cal , Fat: 22.5 g

17. Smoked Beef Brisket

Preparation Time: 20m

Cooking Time: 4-6 hours

Serving: 15

Ingredients:

- 10 lbs. beef brisket
- Mustard
- 1-cup cider vinegar
- Barbecue sauce
- Black Pepper
- Salt

Directions:

1. You should light your smoker to 100°C / 210°F and let it heat for few minutes. Rub the mustard thoroughly on each side of the brisket. You could cut little cracks in the brisket to allow the seasoning to infiltrate the meat to increase the flavor. Then apply all the other seasoning ingredients on both sides of the meat. Put your beef briskets on the smoker, and do not forget to reapply some barbecue sauce on it every occasionally.
2. Beef briskets take some time to smoke! After 4 hours, you will have to check your briskets every hour to see if it is tender and well cooked.
3. Pro tip: Do not cut your smoked beef briskets directly from the smoker. It should rest for about 30 minutes in aluminum foil. This technique will allow the brisket to continue cooking in low temperatures, and the meat will not be rough and hard to cut.

Nutrition: Calories: 641 Protein: 0.7g Vitamin D: 0mcg Calcium: 19mg Iron: 1mg Potassium: 223mg

18. Smoked Beef Roast

Preparation Time: 20m

Cooking Time: 5 hours

Serving: 6

Ingredients:

- 2.7 lbs. beef roast
- One can of beef broth
- 2 tbsps. Garlic
- 2 tbsps. Onion powder
- Salt
- Pepper

Directions:

1. The smoker should be lit to approximately 100°C / 210°F. Lay your beef roast on the smoker, whit its fatty side facing away from the smoker. This will allow the meat juice to infiltrate the pores of the roast. Fill the pan with the broth and keep smoking the beef roast for about 5 hours.

Nutrition: Calories 35, Carbohydrates 4g, Protein 1g, and Fat 2g.

19. Smoked Butt

Preparation Time: 20m

Cooking Time: 6 hours

Serving: 16

Ingredients:

- 8 lbs. pork butt
- 6 tbsps. Yellow mustard
- 2 tbsps. Garlic powder
- 1 tbsp. onion powder
- 1 tbsp. salt
- 1 tbsp. sage, dried
- For the basting:
- ½ c. cider vinegar
- ¼ c. corn oil

- ¼ c. chicken stock
- ¼ c. pineapple concentrate
- 1 tbsp. Paprika
- ½ tbsp. black pepper

Directions:

1. In a bowl, mix the onion powder, sage, salt, and garlic powder.
2. Place the pork in a large zip-lock bag and add mustard.
3. Mix it around, shake it and do whatever it takes so the pork is a coat with mustard. Place in the fridge overnight. In the morning, pat dries using kitchen towels.
4. Preheat the smoker to 250F and use apple and hickory wood chips to lit the charcoal.
5. Place pork on smoker and smoke for 2 hours. Remove from the smoker, baste with marinade, and smoke for 1 hour. Repeat the process once again and smoke for 1 hour. Repeat the process for the third time.
6. Remove pork from the smoker and wrap it in aluminum foil. Place the pork back in the smoker and smoke until the inner temperature reaches 200F.
7. Remove the pork and allow resting for 20 minutes before you serve.

Nutrition: Calories: 334 Cal Fat: 22.5 g Carbs: 6.5 g Protein: 24 g Fiber: 0.1 g

20. Smoked Pork Chops

Preparation Time: 20m

Cooking Time: 2 hours

Serving: 6

Ingredients:

- (6) 6 oz. pork chops
- ½ c. BBQ sauce
- Salt
- Pepper

Directions:

1. Season the chops with pepper and salt.
2. Brush the pork chops with BBQ sauce and place in an electric smoker.
3. Smoke the chops on high for 20 minutes.
4. Reduce heat and continue until the chops reach the desired doneness.

Nutrition: Calories: 334 Cal Fat: 22.5 g Carbs: 6.5 g Protein: 24 g Fiber: 0.1 g

Preparation Time: 20m

Cooking Time: 5 hours

Serving: 6

Ingredients:

- 4 lbs. baby-back ribs
- Salt
- Pepper
- For the espresso sauce:
- 1 ½ tbsps. Olive oil
- ¾ c. honey
- ¾ c. tomato sauce
- 3 tbsps. Soy sauce
- 3 tbsps. Espresso
- 1 ½ tbsps. Garlic, minced

Directions:

1. Prepare the sauce; use a saucepan to mix garlic and olive oil. Cook until fragrant. Tae away from the heat, and on cooling, stir in the remaining ingredients. Simmer for 15 minutes and take away from the heat.
2. Generously season the pork ribs with salt and pepper.
3. Preheat smoker to 225F. Use the hickory chips for the first two hours.
4. Smoke the ribs for 3 hours. After 3 hours, baste the ribs with prepared espresso sauce and wrap them in a heavy-duty aluminum foil.
5. Continue smoking for 1 ½ hour more or until inner temperature reaches 160F.

Nutrition: Calories: 334 Cal Fat: 22.5 g Carbs: 6.5 g Protein: 24 g Fiber: 0.1 g

Poultry Recipes

22. Lemon Chicken Breast

Preparation Time: 15 minutes | Cooking Time: 30 minutes | Servings: 4

Ingredients:

Six chicken breasts, skinless and boneless

½ cup oil

1-3 fresh thyme sprigs

One teaspoon ground black pepper

Two teaspoon salt

Two teaspoons honey

One garlic clove, chopped

One lemon, juiced and zested

Lemon wedges

Directions:

Take a bowl and prepare the marinade by mixing thyme, pepper, salt, honey, garlic, lemon zest, and juice. Mix well until dissolved

Add oil and whisk

Clean breasts and pat them dry, place in a bag alongside marinade, and let them sit in the fridge for 4 hours

Preheat your smoker to 400 degrees F

Drain chicken and smoke until the internal temperature reaches 165 degrees, for about 15 minutes

Serve and enjoy!

Nutrition:

Calories: 230 | Fats: 7g | Carbs: 1g | Fiber: 2g

23. Paprika Chicken

Preparation Time: 20 minutes | Cooking Time: 2 – 4 hours | Servings: 7

Ingredients:

4-6 chicken breast

Four tablespoons olive oil

Two tablespoons smoked paprika

½ tablespoon salt

¼ teaspoon pepper

Two teaspoons garlic powder

Two teaspoons garlic salt

Two teaspoons pepper

One teaspoon cayenne pepper

One teaspoon rosemary

Directions:

Preheat your smoker to 220 degrees Fahrenheit using your favorite wood Pellets

Prepare your chicken breast according to your desired shapes and transfer to a greased baking dish

Take a medium bowl and add spices, stir well

Press the spice mix over the chicken and transfer the chicken to the smoker

Smoke for 1-1 and a ½ hours

Turn-over and cook for 30 minutes more

Once the internal temperature reaches 165 degrees Fahrenheit

Remove from the smoker and cover with foil

Allow it to rest for 15 minutes

Enjoy!

Nutrition:

Calories: 237 | Fats: 6.1g | Carbs: 14g | Fiber: 3g

Preparation Time: 15 minutes | Cooking Time: 8 hours | Servings: 6

Ingredients:

2 lbs. Turkey breast

4 cups Cold water

¼ cup Salt

1 cup Brown sugar

2 tbsp. Garlic powder

1 tbsp. Sea salt

1 tbsp. Cayenne pepper

2 tbsp. dried onions

2 tbsps. Sugar

2 tbsps. Chili powder

2 tbsps. Black pepper

2 tbsps. Cumin

¼ cup Paprika

2 tbsps. Brown sugar

Directions:

In a large enough bowl, mix all of the brine ingredients except the turkey.

Add the turkey and cover with brine properly. Put this bowl in your refrigerator for about 15–20 hours.

Remove the turkey from the mixture of brine.

Prepare your Wood Pellet Smoker-Grill by preheating it to a temperature of about 180°F. Close the lid for about 15 minutes before adding the turkey.

Prepare the BBQ rub with the provided ingredients and coat the turkey properly.

Transfer this seasoned turkey straight to the grilling grate.

Allow for about 6–8 hours of smoking to get an internal temperature of about 160°F.

Remove the smoked turkey from your smoker grill and allow it to rest for at least 10 minutes.

Nutrition:

Calories: 155 | Protein: 29g | Carbs: 8g | Fat: 3g

Preparation Time: 30 minutes | Cooking Time: 6 hours | Servings: 8

Ingredients:

Two t. thyme

Two t. sage

½ c. apple juice

One stick melted butter

¼ c. poultry seasoning

EVOO

10-12-pound turkey

Directions:

Add wood pellets to your smoker and follow your cooker's startup procedure. Preheat your smoker, with your lid closed, until it reaches 250.

Rub the oil and seasoning on the turkey. Get some in under the skin as well as inside.

Mix the thyme, sage, juice, and butter.

Place the turkey in a roasting pan, put it on the grill, cover, and cook for 5-6 hours. Baste it every hour with the juice mixture.

It should reach 165. Let it rest for 15-20 minutes before carving.

Nutrition:

Calories: 48.2 | Protein: 8.3g | Carbs: 0.3g | Fat: 1.4g

26. Pineapple Turkey Wings

Preparation Time: 30 minutes | Cooking Time: 6 hours | Servings: 6

Ingredients:

Pepper

Salt

¼ t. garlic powder

Two pounds turkey wings

One t. packed brown sugar

Two t. chili powder

One 11-ounce can pineapple, undrained

¼ t. ground ginger

One 11-ounce-can of tomato sauce

Directions:

Put the turkey wings into a large dish. Make sure they are in one layer. Put the pepper, salt, garlic powder, ginger, chili powder, brown sugar, pineapple, and tomato sauce in a bowl.

This mixture should be poured on the turkey. Place into the refrigerator for four to five hours.

Add wood pellets to your smoker and follow your cooker's startup procedure.

Preheat your smoker, with your lid closed, until it reaches 350. Take the turkey wings out of the marinade.

Use the paper towels to pat them dry. Place them onto the grill and smoke for 5 minutes on both sides.

Move to the cool side and allow to smoke for an additional 40 minutes. Internal temperature needs to be 165.

Nutrition:

Calories: 260 | Protein: 31.05g | Carbs: 0.1g | Fat: 14.1g

27. Barbecue Chicken Breasts

Preparation Time: 20 minutes | Cooking Time: 30 minutes | Servings: 4

Ingredients:

Two t. Worcestershire sauce

½ c. hot barbecue sauce

One c. barbecue sauce

Two cloves minced garlic

¼ c. olive oil

Four chicken breasts

Directions:

Put the chicken breasts into a deep container.

In another bowl, put the Worcestershire sauce, barbecue sauces, garlic, and olive oil. Stir well to combine.

Use half to marinate the chicken and reserve the rest for basting.

Add wood pellets to your smoker and follow your cooker's startup procedure. Preheat your smoker, with your lid closed, until it reaches 350.

Take the chicken breasts out of the sauce. On the grill, place them before smoking them for approximately 20 minutes.

About ten minutes before the chicken is finished, baste with reserved barbecue sauce.

Nutrition:

Calories: 220 | Protein: 27g | Carbs: 19g | Fat: 3.3g

28. BBQ Chicken Nachos

Ingredients:

- 1-1/4 Lbs. Chicken Breasts, Boneless, Skinless
- Traeger Pork & Poultry Rub, As Needed
- 1/2 To 3/4 Cup Traeger Qu BBQ Sauce
- 24 Large Tortilla Chips
- 3 Cups Mexican Blend Shredded Cheese
- 1/2 cup Black Olives, Sliced and Drained
- Pickled Jalapenos, Sliced
- 3 Scallions, Thinly Sliced
- 1 cup Sour Cream

Instructions:

- Season the chicken breasts with the Traeger Pork and Poultry Rub.
- When ready to cook, set temperature to 350°F and preheat, lid closed for 15 minutes.
- Arrange the chicken breasts on the grill grate and cook, turning once halfway through the cooking time, for 25 to 30 minutes, or until the internal temperature when read on an instant-read meat thermometer is 170°F. Transfer to a cutting board and let rest for 3 minutes. Leave the grill on if you are making the nachos immediately.
- Dice the chicken into small cubes, 1/2-inch or less. Transfer to a mixing bowl and pour 1/2 cup of Traeger Regular Barbecue Sauce over the diced chicken. Stir gently to coat each piece.
- Set aside, or cover and refrigerate if not making the nachos immediately. Lay the tortilla chips in a single layer on a rimmed baking sheet or pizza pan. Sprinkle evenly with half the cheese and a few of the jalapenos (if using).
- Spoon barbecued chicken mixture on each chip. Top with black olives and more pickled jalapeno, if desired. Sprinkle the remaining half of the cheese evenly over the chips. Scatter the sliced onions over the chips.
- Put the baking sheet on the grill grate. Bake until the chips are crisp and the cheese is melted for 12 to 15 minutes. With a spatula, transfer the nachos to a plate or platter. Serve immediately with sour cream and pickled jalapenos. Enjoy!

29. Tandoori Chicken Wings

Preparation Time: 20 minutes

Cooking Time: 1 hour 20 minutes

Servings: 4-6

Ingredients:

- 1/4 cup yogurt
- One whole scallion, minced
- One tablespoon minced cilantro leaves
- Two teaspoons ginger, minced
- One teaspoon masala
- One teaspoon salt
- One teaspoon ground black pepper
- 1 1/2 pounds chicken wings
- Two tablespoons mayonnaise
- Two tablespoons cucumber
- Two teaspoons lemon juice
- 1/2 teaspoon cumin
- 1/2 teaspoon salt

- 1/8 cayenne pepper

Directions:

1. Combine yogurt, scallion, ginger, gram masala, salt, cilantro, and pepper ingredients in the jar of a blender and process until smooth.

2. Put chicken and massage the bag to cat all the wings

3. Refrigerate for 4 to 8 hours. Remove the excess marinade from the wings; discard the marinade

4. Arrange the wings on the grill. Cook at 200°F for 50 minutes or until the skins are brown and crisp and meat is no longer pink at the bone.

5. Meanwhile, combine all sauce ingredients; set aside, and refrigerate until ready to serve.

6. When wings are cooked through, transfer to a plate or platter. Serve with yogurt sauce

Nutrition:

Calories: 241

Carbohydrates: 11 g

Protein: 12 g

Fat: 16 g

Saturated fat: 3 g

30. Smoke Roasted Chicken

Preparation Time: 20 minutes

Cooking Time: 1 hour 20 minutes

Servings: 4-6

Ingredients:

- Eight tablespoons butter, room temperature
- One clove garlic, minced
- One scallion, minced
- Two tablespoons of fresh herbs such as thyme, rosemary, sage, or parsley
- Chicken rub as needed
- Lemon juice
- As needed, vegetable oil

Directions:

1. In a small cooking bowl, mix the scallions, garlic, butter, minced fresh herbs, 1-1/2 teaspoon of the rub, and lemon juice. Mix with a spoon.

2. Removed any giblets from the cavity of the chicken. Wash the chicken inside and out with cold running water. Dry thoroughly with paper towels.

3. Sprinkle a generous amount of Chicken Rub inside the cavity of the chicken.

4. Gently loosen the skin around the chicken breast and slide in a few tablespoons of the herb butter under the skin, and cover.

5. Cover the outside with the remaining herb butter.

6. Insert the chicken wings behind the back. Tie both legs together with a butcher's string.

7. Powder the outside of the chicken with more Chicken Rub, then insert sprigs of fresh herbs inside the cavity of the chicken.

8. Set temperature to High and preheat at 200°F, lid closed for 15 minutes.

9. Oil the grill with vegetable oil. Move the chicken on the grill grate, breast-side up, then close the lid.

10. After the chicken has cooked for 1 hour, lift the lid. If chicken is browning too quickly, cover the breast and legs with aluminum foil.

11. Close the lid, then continue to roast the chicken until an instant-read meat thermometer inserted into the thickest part registers a temperature of 165F

12. Take off the chicken from the grill and let rest for 5 minutes. Serve, Enjoy!

Nutrition:

Calories: 222 kcal

Carbohydrates: 11 g

Protein: 29 g

Fat: 4 g

Cholesterol: 62 mg

Sodium: 616 mg

Potassium: 620 mg

31. Grilled Asian Chicken Burgers

Preparation Time: 5 minutes

Cooking Time: 50 minutes

Servings: 4-6

Ingredients:

- 2-pound chicken, ground

- 1 cup panko breadcrumbs

- 1 cup parmesan cheese

- One small jalapeno, diced

- Two whole scallions, minced

- Two garlic clove

- 1/4 cup minced cilantro leaves

- Two tablespoons mayonnaise

- Two tablespoons chili sauce

- One tablespoon soy sauce

- One tablespoon ginger, minced

- Two teaspoons lemon juice

- Two teaspoons lemon zest

- One teaspoon salt

- One teaspoon ground black pepper

- Eight hamburger buns

- One tomato, sliced

- Arugula, fresh

- One red onion sliced

Directions:

1. Align a rimmed baking sheet with aluminum foil, then spray with nonstick cooking spray.

2. In a large bowl, combine the chicken, jalapeno, scallion, garlic, cilantro, panko, Parmesan, chili sauce, soy sauce, ginger, mayonnaise, lemon juice, and zest, and salt and pepper.

3. Work the mixture with your fingers until the ingredients are well combined. If the mixture looks too wet to form patties and add additional panko.

4. Wash your hands under cold running water, form the meat into eight patties, each about an inch larger than the buns and ¾" thick. Use your thumbs or a tablespoon, make a wide, shallow depression in the top of each

5. Put them on the prepared baking sheet. Spray the tops with nonstick cooking spray.

6. Set the pellet grill to 350°F, then preheat for 15 minutes, lid closed.

7. Order the burgers on the grilled grate; removed and discard foil on the baking sheet.

8. Grilled the burgers for about 25 to 30 minutes, turning once or until they release easily from the grill grate when a clean metal spatula is slipped under them. The internal temperature when read on an instant-read meat thermometer should be 160°F.

9. Spread mayonnaise and arrange a tomato slice, if desired, and a few arugulas leave on one-half of each bun. Top with a grilled burger and red onions, then replace the top half of the bun. Serve immediately. Enjoy

Nutrition:

Calories: 329 kcal

Carbohydrates: 10 g

Protein: 21 g

Fat: 23 g

32. Smoked Turkey

Preparation Time: 8 hours

Cooking Time: 5 hours

Servings: 6-8

Ingredients:

- One turkey (12 to 14 lb.) thawed or fresh, excess skin trimmed

- ¾ lb. butter, unsalted

- Brine:

- 2 gallons water and ice

- cups of sugar

- 2 cups salt

- Rub:

- 1/2 cup black pepper, ground

- 1/2 cup salt

Directions:

1. One day before you want to cook the turkey, preparation time is it for bringing.

2. In a saucepan, combine the sugar and salt. Add water and let it boil until dissolved. Pour the mixture into a big bucket and add water and ice 2 gallons.

3. Put the turkey in the brine and if it starts to float, place a large plate on top so that it stays submerged, cover the bucket and refrigerate until the next day.

4. Preheat the grill 180°F with the lid closed.

5. Remove the turkey and make sure the cavity is also empty of brine. Place the turkey on a piece of a cooking sheet.

6. Sprinkle and rub black pepper and salt on the whole turkey but not inside.

7. Cook on the grill for 2 hours. After 2 hours, increase the temperature to 225°F and cook one more hour. Increase again to 325°F. When the color of the turkey is according to your taste, could you place it in a pan? Cut the unsalted butter into squares and place it on the meat.

8. Wrap the turkey in a foil and cook on the grill until it reaches 165°F (breast) internal temperature and the thigh 180°F (as read by a meat thermometer).

9. Let it rest for 30 minutes and serve.

Nutrition:

Calories: 380

Proteins: 40 g

Carbohydrates: 3 g

Fat: 16 g

33. Apple Smoked Turkey

Preparation Time: 30 minutes

Cooking Time: 3 hours

Servings: 5

Ingredients:

- 4 cups Apple wood chips

- One fresh or frozen turkey of about 12 pounds

- Three tablespoons of extra-virgin olive oil

- One tablespoon of chopped fresh sage

- 2 and 1/2 teaspoons of kosher salt

- Two teaspoons of freshly ground black pepper

- 1 and 1/2 teaspoons of paprika

- One teaspoon of chopped fresh thyme

- One teaspoon of chopped fresh oregano

- One teaspoon of garlic powder

- 1 cup of water

- 1/2 cup of chopped onion

- 1/2 cup of chopped carrot

- 1/2 cup of chopped celery

Directions:

1. Soak the wood chips into the water for about 1 hour, then drain very well.

2. Removed neck and the giblets from the turkey; then reserve and discard the liver. Pat the turkey dry; then trim any excess of fat and start at the neck's cavity.

3. Loosen the skin from the breast and the drumstick by inserting your fingers, gently pushing it between the meat and skin, lifting the wingtips, then over the back, and tuck under the turkey.

4. Combine the oil and the next seven ingredients in a medium bowl, rub the oil under the skin, then rub it over the breasts and the drumsticks.

5. Tie the legs with the kitchen string.

6. Pour 1 cup of water, the onion, the carrot, and the celery into the bottom of an aluminum foil roasting pan.

7. Place the roasting rack into a pan; then arrange the turkey with the breast side up over a roasting rack; then let stand at room temperature for about 1 hour.

8. Remove the grill rack; then preheat the charcoal smoker grill to medium-high heat.

9. Preheat, the smoker to a temperature of about 225°F.

10. Place 2 cups of wood chips on the heating element on the right side.

11. Replace the grill rack; then place the roasting pan with the turkey over the grill rack over the left burner.

12. Cover and smoke for about 3 hours, turn the chicken halfway through the cooking time, then add the remaining 2 cups of wood chips halfway through the cooking time.

13. Place the turkey over a cutting board; then let stand for about 30 minutes.

14. Discard the turkey skin, then serve and enjoy your dish!

Nutrition:

Calories: 530

Fat: 22 g

Carbohydrates: 14 g

Protein: 41 g

Dietary Fiber: 2 g

34. Porchetta

Preparation Time: 30 minutes

Cooking Time: 3 hours

Servings: 12

Ingredients:

- 6 pounds skin-on pork belly
- 4 pounds center-cut pork loin
- 4 tbsps. olive oil
- 1 cup apple juice
- Two garlic cloves (minced)
- One onion (diced)
- 1 1/4 cups grated pecorino
- 1 tsp. ground black pepper
- 2 tsp. Kosher salt - 3 tbsps. fennel seeds
- 1 tbsp. freshly chopped rosemary
- 1 tbsp. freshly chopped sage
- 1 tbsp. freshly chopped thyme
- 1 tbsp. grated lemon zest

Rub:

- 1 tbsp. Chili powder - 2 tsp. grilling seasoning
- 1 tsp. salt or to taste
- 1/2 tsp. cayenne
- 1 tsp. Oregano - 1 tsp. paprika
- 1 tsp. mustard powder

Directions:

1. Butterfly the pork loin and place it in the middle of two plastic wraps. On a flat surface, pound the pork evenly until it is 1/2 inch thick.

2. Set all the rub ingredients in a small mixing bowl.

3. Place the butterflied pork on a flat surface, cut side up. Season the cut side generously with 1/3 of the rub.

4. Heat 1 tbsp. Olive oil in your frying pan over medium to high heat. Add the onion, garlic, and fennel seed. Sauté until the veggies are tender.

5. Stir the black pepper, 1 tsp. Kosher salt, and rosemary, sage, and thyme, and lemon zest. Cook for 1 minute and stir in the cheese.

6. Put the sautéed ingredients on the flat pork and spread evenly. Roll up the pork like you are rolling a burrito.

7. Brush the rolled pork loin with 1 Tbsp. Oil and season with the remaining rub. The loin with butcher's string at the 1-inch interval.

8. Roll the pork belly around the pork, skin side out. Brush the pork belly with the remaining oil and season with 1 tsp. Salt.

9. Bring a rack into a roasting pan device and place the Porchetta on the rack. Pour the wine into the bottom of the roasting pan.

10.   Start your grill on smoke mode, leaving the lid open for 5 minutes until the fire starts.

11.   Close the lid and preheat the grill to 325°F, using maple or apple hardwood pellets.

12.   Place the roasting pan on the grill and roast Porchetta for about 3 hours or until the Porchetta's internal temperature reaches 155°F, as read by a meat thermometer.

13.   Remove the Porchetta from heat and let it rest for a few minutes to cool.

14.   Remove the butcher's string. Slice Porchetta into sizes and serve.

Nutrition:

Calories: 611

Fat: 22.7 g

Cholesterol: 252 mg

Carbohydrate: 6.6 g

Protein: 89.4 g

35. Ham and Cheese Stuffed Baked Chicken

Preparation Time: 15 minutes

Cooking Time: 58 minutes

Servings: 6

Ingredients:

- All-purpose flour — 1/3 cup

- Chicken breasts — 4, no bones, no skin, and tenders removed

- Parmesan cheese — ¼ cup, finely grated

- Salt — according to taste

- Black pepper — according to taste

- Ham slices — 8, thin

- Thyme leaves — 2 tablespoons

- Melted butter — 2 tbsps.

- Breadcrumbs — 1 cup, dried

- Baby spinach — 1 cup

- Eggs — 2

Mozzarella cheese — 2 cups

Directions:

1. Use parchment paper to line a large enough baking dish. Set aside. Put each chicken breast on a piece of plastic wrap and cover it with another piece. Then, pound the breasts evenly without breaking the chicken.
2. Remove from the plastic wrap and make chicken rolls by adding ham slices, spinach, and cheese to every flattened chicken breast. Seal properly

and cover in new plastic wrap to store in the refrigerator for about 60 minutes.

3. You can put some flour in a baking dish and season it with pepper and salt during this time. In a different dish, add Parmesan, breadcrumbs, thyme, and butter and mix properly. In another dish, beat the eggs.

4. Now, you have different stations of the flour mixture, eggs, and breadcrumb mixture. Remove the chicken rolls and coat them with flour, then eggs, and, finally, breadcrumbs. Lay all the coated chicken rolls in a large enough baking dish.

5. Prepare your Wood Pellet Smoker-Grill by preheating it to a temperature of about 350°F. Close the top lid for 12–18 minutes.

6. Transfer the baking dish straight to your grilling grate and bake for about 30–32 minutes. Take out, slice, and serve.

Nutrition:

Calories: 271   Protein: 40g Carbs: 6g Fat: 9g

36. Barbecue Chicken Breasts

Preparation Time: 20 minutes

Cooking Time: 30 minutes

Servings: 4

Ingredients:

- Two T. Worcestershire sauce

- ½ c. hot barbecue sauce

- One c. barbecue sauce

- Two cloves minced garlic

- ¼ c. olive oil

- 4 chicken breasts

Directions:

1. Put the chicken breasts into a deep container.
2. In another bowl, put the Worcestershire sauce, barbecue sauces, garlic, and olive oil. Stir well to combine.
3. Use half to marinate the chicken and reserve the rest for basting.
4. Add wood pellets to your smoker and follow your cooker's startup procedure. Preheat your smoker, with your lid closed, until it reaches 350.
5. Take the chicken breasts out of the sauce. On the grill, place them before smoking them for approximately 20 minutes.
6. About ten minutes before the chicken is finished, baste with reserved barbecue sauce.

Nutrition:

Calories: 220   Protein: 27g Carbs: 19g Fat: 3.3g

37. Cilantro-Lime Chicken

Preparation Time: 50 minutes

Cooking Time: 5 hours

Servings: 4

Ingredients:

- Pepper
- Salt
- four cloves minced garlic
- ½ c. lime juice
- One c. honey
- Two T. olive oil
- ½ c. chopped cilantro
- 4 chicken breasts

Directions:

1. Put the chicken breasts into a large zip-top bag.
2. Put the pepper, salt, olive oil, garlic, honey, lime juice, and cilantro in another bowl. Stir well to combine.
3. Use half as a marinade and reserve the rest for later.
4. Place into the refrigerator for four to five hours.
5. Add wood pellets to your smoker and follow your cooker's startup procedure. Preheat your smoker, with your lid closed, until it reaches 350.
6. Remove the chicken breasts from the bag. Use paper towels to pat them dry. Let them smoke up in the grill for about fifteen minutes
7. About five minutes before the chicken is finished, baste with reserved marinade.

Nutrition:

Calories: 62.5   Protein: 8.2g Carbs: 3g Fat: 2g

38. Lemon Honey Chicken

Preparation Time: 30 minutes

Cooking Time: 30 minutes

Servings: 4

Ingredients:

·   Pepper

·   Salt

·   Chopped rosemary

·   One clove of crushed garlic

·   One T. honey

·   Juice of one lemon

·   ½ c. chicken broth

·   3 T. butter

- 4 chicken breasts

Directions:

1. Place a pan on the stove and melt the butter. Place chicken breasts into hot butter and sear on each side until a nice color has formed.
2. Take out of the pan and allow to rest for ten minutes.
3. In a small bowl, put the pepper, salt, rosemary, garlic, honey, lemon juice, and broth. Stir well to combine.
4. Rub each breast with the honey lemon mixture.
5. Add wood pellets to your smoker and follow your cooker's startup procedure. Preheat your smoker, with your lid closed, until it reaches 350.
6. Put the chicken breasts onto the preheated grill and grill for 20 minutes.

Nutrition:

Calories: 265.1   Protein: 31.1g Carbs: 25.3g Fat: 7g

39. Delicious Soy Marinated Steak

Preparation time: 20 minutes

Cooking time: 55 minutes

Servings: 4

Ingredients:

- 1/2 chopped onion

- .3 chopped cloves of garlic
- 1/4 cup of olive oil
- 1/4 cup of balsamic vinegar
- 1/4 cup of soy sauce
- One tablespoon of Dijon mustard
- One tablespoon of rosemary
- One teaspoon of salt to taste
- 1/2 teaspoon of ground black pepper to taste
- 1 1/2 pounds of flank steak

Intolerances:

- Gluten-Free
- Egg-Free
- Lactose-Free

Directions:

1. Using a large mixing bowl, add all the ingredients on the list aside from the steak, then mix properly to combine.
2. Place the steak in a Ziploc bag, pour in the prepared marinade then shake properly to coat.
3. Place the bag in the refrigerator and let the steak marinate for about thirty minutes to two full days.
4. Preheat the Wood Pellet Smoker and Grill to 350-400°F, remove the steak from its marinade, then set the marinade aside for blasting.
5. Place the steak on the preheated grill, then grill for about six to eight minutes until the beef is heated through.
6. Flip the steak over and cook for an additional six minutes until an inserted thermometer reads 150°F.
7. Place the steak on a cutting board and let rest for about five minutes. Slice and serve.

Nutrition:

- Calories: 300
- Fat: 20g
- Carbs: 8g
- Protein: 22g

40. Grilled Steak and Vegetable Kebabs

Preparation time: 15 minutes

Cooking time: 20 minutes

Servings: 5

Ingredients:

Marinade

- 1/4 cup of olive oil
- 1/4 cup of soy sauce
- 1 1/2 tablespoons of fresh lemon juice
- 1 1/2 tablespoons of red wine vinegar
- 2 1/2 tablespoons of Worcestershire sauce
- One tablespoon of honey
- Two teaspoons of Dijon mustard
- One tablespoon of garlic

- One teaspoon of freshly ground black pepper to taste

Kebabs

- 1 3/4 lbs. of sirloin steak
- One sliced zucchini.
- Three sliced bell peppers
- One large and sliced red onion
- One tablespoon of olive oil
- Salt and freshly ground black pepper to taste
- 1/2 teaspoon of garlic powder

Intolerances:

- Gluten-Free
- Egg-Free
- Lactose-Free

Directions:

1. Using a large mixing bowl, add in the oil, soy sauce, lemon juice, red wine vinegar, Worcestershire sauce, Dijon, honey, garlic, and pepper to taste, then mix properly to combine.
2. Using a sharp knife, cut the steak into smaller pieces or cubes, then add to a resealable bag.
3. Pour the marinade into the bag with steak, then shake to coat. Let the steak marinate for about three to six hours in the refrigerator.
4. Preheat the Wood Pellet Smoker and Grill to 425°F, place the veggies into a mixing bowl, add in oil, garlic powder, salt, and pepper to taste, then mix to combine.
5. Thread the veggies and steak alternately unto skewers, place the skewers on the preheated grill, and grill for about eight to nine minutes until it is cooked through.
6. Make sure you turn the kebabs occasionally as you cook. Serve.

Nutrition:

- Calories: 350
- Fat: 14g
- Carbs: 18g
- Protein: 34g

41. Grilled Barbecue Beef Ribs

Preparation time: 30 minutes

Cooking time: 1 hour

Servings: 4

Ingredients:

- 1/2 cup of Dijon mustard
- Two tablespoons of cider vinegar
- 3 lbs. of spareribs
- Four tablespoons of paprika powder
- 1/2 tablespoon of chili powder
- 1 1/2 tablespoon of garlic powder
- Two teaspoons of ground cumin
- Two teaspoons of onion powder

- 1 1/2 tablespoon of ground black pepper to taste
- Two tablespoons of salt to taste
- Two tablespoons of butter, which is optional

Intolerances:

- Gluten-Free
- Egg-Free
- Lactose-Free

Directions:

1. Preheat a Wood Pellet Smoker and Grill to 350°F, use a small mixing bowl, add in the mustard and the vinegar, and mix properly to combine.
2. Rub the mixture on the spareribs, coating all sides. Using another mixing bowl, add in the paprika powder, chili powder, garlic powder, cumin, onion powder, salt, and pepper to taste and mix properly.
3. Reserve a small quantity of the mixture, seasoned the spareribs with the rest of the spice mixture, coating all sides.
4. Wrap the seasoned ribs in aluminum foil, top with the butter if desired, then place the ribs on the preheated grill.
5. Grill the ribs for about one hour until it is cooked through. Make sure you flip after every twenty minutes.
6. Once the ribs are cooked through, remove from the grill, unwrap the aluminum foil, then grill the ribs for another two to five minutes until crispy.
7. Let the ribs cool for a few minutes, slice, and serve.

Nutrition:

- Calories: 280
- Fat: 42g
- Cholesterol: 94mg
- Carbs: 6g
- Protein: 55g

42. Garlic Butter Grilled Steak

Preparation time: 15 minutes

Cooking time: 25 minutes

Servings: 4

Ingredients:

- Three tablespoons of unsalted butter
- Four cloves of garlic
- One tablespoon of chopped parsley
- One tablespoon of olive oil
- Four strip steaks
- Salt and pepper to taste

Intolerances:

- Gluten-Free
- Egg-Free
- Lactose-Free

Directions:

1. Using a large mixing bowl, add in the butter, garlic, and parsley, then mix properly to combine, set aside in the refrigerator.
2. Preheat a Wood Pellet Smoker and Grill to 400° F, use paper towels to pat the steak dry, rub oil on all sides, then season with some sprinkles of salt and pepper to taste.
3. Place the seasoned steak on the preheated grill and grill for about four to five minutes.
4. Flip the steak over and grill for an additional four to five minutes until it becomes brown and cooked as desired.
5. Rub the steak with the butter mixture, heat on the grill for a few minutes, slice and serve.

Nutrition:

- Calories: 543
- Fat: 25g
- Carbs: 1g
- Protein: 64g

43. Grilled Coffee Rub Brisket

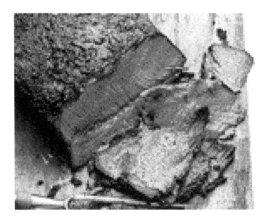

Preparation time: 30 minutes

Cooking time: 15 hours

Servings: 4

Ingredients:

- 1 (14 pounds) whole brisket
- Coffee Rub
- Two tablespoons of coarse salt to taste
- Two tablespoons of instant coffee
- Two tablespoons of garlic powder
- Two tablespoons of smoked paprika
- One tablespoon of pepper to taste
- One tablespoon of crushed coriander
- One tablespoon of onion powder
- One teaspoon of chili powder
- 1/2 teaspoon of cayenne

Intolerances:

- Gluten-Free
- Egg-Free
- Lactose-Free

Directions:

1. Using a large mixing bowl, add in the instant coffee, garlic powder, paprika, coriander, onion powder, chili powder, cayenne, salt, and pepper to taste, then mix properly to combine.
2. Rub the brisket with the prepared rub, coating all sides, then set aside.
3. Preheat a Wood Pellet Smoker and Grill to 225°F, add in the seasoned brisket, cover the smoker, and smoke for about eight hours until a thermometer reads 165°For the briskets.

4. Place the brisket in an aluminum foil, then wrap up. Place the foil-wrapped brisket on the wood Pellet smoker and cook for another five to eight hours until the meat reaches an internal temperature of 225ºF.
5. Once cooked, let the brisket rest on the cutting board for about one hour, slice against the grain then serve.

Nutrition:

- Calories: 420
- Fat: 11g
- Cholesterol: 100mg
- Carbs: 15g

44. Grilled Herb Steak

Preparation time: 15 minutes

Cooking time: 20 minutes

Servings: 4

Ingredients:

- One tablespoon of peppercorns
- One teaspoon of fennel seeds
- Three large and minced cloves of garlic

- Two teaspoons of kosher salt to taste
- One tablespoon of chopped rosemary
- One tablespoon of chopped thyme
- Two teaspoons of black pepper to taste
- Two teaspoons of olive oil
- 1 pound of flank steak

Intolerances:

- Gluten-Free
- Egg-Free
- Lactose-Free

Directions:

1. Using a grinder or a food processor, add in the peppercorns, and the fennel seeds, then blend until completely crushed, then add to a mixing bowl.
2. Add in the garlic, rosemary, thyme, salt, and pepper to taste, mix properly to combine, and set aside.
3. Rub the steak with oil, coating all sides, then coat with half of the peppercorn mixture. Make sure the steak is coated all around.
4. Place the steak in a Ziploc plastic bag, then let marinate in the refrigerator for about 2 to 8 minutes.
5. Preheat a Wood Pellet Smoker and Grill to 450°F, place the coated steak on the grill and cook for about five to six minutes.
6. Flip the steak over and cook for another five to six minutes until cooked through.
7. Once cooked, let the steak cool for a few minutes, slice, and serve.

Nutrition.

- Calories: 440
- Fat: 25g
- Cholesterol: 90mg

- Carbs: 20g
- Protein: 35g

45. BBQ Meatloaf

Preparation time: 25 minutes

Cooking time: 1 hour and 30 minutes

Servings: 4

Ingredients:

- 1 1/2 pounds of ground beef
- 1/3 cup of ketchup
- Two teaspoons of Worcestershire sauce
- One large egg
- 1 cup of soft breadcrumbs
- 1 cup of chopped onions
- 1/2 teaspoon of salt to taste
- 1/4 teaspoon of ground black pepper to taste
- Barbecue sauce for a glaze

Intolerances:

- Lactose-Free

Directions:

1. Preheat a Wood Pellet Smoker and Grill to 350°F, using a large mixing bowl, add in the beef alongside the rest of the ingredients on the list (aside from the barbecue sauce), then mix properly to combine.
2. Place the beef mixture in an aluminum foil, then form it into your desired loaf shape.
3. Unfold the foil, brush the meatloaf with barbecue sauce, then warp in.
4. Place the meatloaf on the grill and cook for about 1 hour to 1 hour and 30 minutes until it attains a temperature of 160°F.
5. Slice and serve.

Nutrition:

- Calories: 370
- Fat: 15g
- Carbs: 20g
- Protein: 35g

Fish & Seafood Recipes

46. Sweet Honey Soy Smoked Salmon

Preparation time: 15 minutes

Cooking time: 2 hours and 10 minutes

Servings: 10

Ingredients:

- Salmon fillet (4-lbs., 1.8-kg.)

The Brine:

- ¾ cup Brown sugar
- 3 tbsp. Soy sauce
- 3 tsp. Kosher salt
- 3 cups Coldwater

The Glaze:

- 2 tbsp. Butter
- 2 tbsp. Brown sugar
- 2 tbsp. Olive oil
- 2 tbsp. Honey
- 1 tbsp. Soy sauce

The Heat:

- Alder wood pellets

Directions:

1. Add brown sugar, soy sauce, and kosher salt to the cold water, then stir until dissolved.

2. Put the salmon fillet into the brine mixture and soak it for at least 2 hours.

3. After 2 hours, take the salmon fillet out of the brine, then wash and rinse it.

4. Plug the wood pellet smoker and place the wood pellet inside the hopper. Turn the switch on.

5. Set the temperature to 225°F (107°C) and prepare the wood pellet smoker for indirect heat. Wait until the wood pellet smoker is ready.

6. Place the salmon fillet in the wood pellet smoker and smoke it for 2 hours.

7. In the meantime, melt the butter over low heat, then mix it with brown sugar, olive oil, honey, and soy sauce. Mix well.

8. After an hour of smoking, baste the glaze mixture over the salmon fillet and repeat it once every 10 minutes.

9. Smoke until the salmon is flaky and remove it from the wood pellet smoker.

10. Transfer the smoked salmon fillet to a serving dish and baste the remaining glaze mixture over it.

11. Serve and enjoy.

Nutrition:

- Amount per 199 g
- = 1 serving(s)

- Energy (calories): 345 kcal
- Protein: 37.42 g
- Fat: 15.6 g
- Carbohydrates: 11.52 g

47. Cranberry Lemon Smoked Mackerel

Preparation time: 15 minutes

Cooking time: 2 hours and 10 minutes

Servings: 10

Ingredients:

- Mackerel fillet (3.5-lb., 2.3-kg.)

The Brine:

- Three cans of cranberry juice
- ½ cup pineapple juice
- 3 cups cold water
- ¼ cup brown sugar
- Two cinnamon stick
- Two fresh lemons
- Two bay leaves

- Three fresh thyme leaves

The Rub:

- ¾ tsp. kosher salt
- ¾ tsp. pepper

The Heat:

- Alder wood pellets

Directions:

1. Mix the cranberry juice and pineapple juice with water, then stir well.

2. Stir in brown sugar to the liquid mixture, then mix until dissolved.

3. Cut the lemons into slices, then add them to the liquid mixture and cinnamon sticks, bay leaves, and fresh thyme leaves.

4. Put the mackerel fillet into the brine and soak it for at least 2 hours. Store it in the refrigerator to keep the mackerel fillet fresh.

5. After 2 hours, remove the mackerel fillet from the refrigerator and take it out of the brine mixture.

6. Plug the wood pellet smoker and place the wood pellet inside the hopper. Turn the switch on.

7. Set the temperature to 225°F (107°C) and prepare the wood pellet smoker for indirect heat. Wait until the wood pellet smoker is ready.

8. Sprinkle salt and pepper over the mackerel fillet, then place it in the wood pellet smoker.

9. Smoke the mackerel fillet for 2 hours or until it flakes and removes it from the wood pellet smoker.

10. Transfer the smoked mackerel fillet to a serving dish and serve.

11. Enjoy!

Nutrition:

- Amount per 225 g
- = 1 serving(s)
- Energy (calories): 386 kcal
- Protein: 46.11 g
- Fat: 4.56 g
- Carbohydrates: 37.85 g

48. Citrusy Smoked Tuna Belly with Sesame Aroma

Preparation time: 15 minutes

Cooking time: 2 hours and 10 minutes

Servings: 10

Ingredients:

- Tuna belly (4-lbs., 1.8-kg.)

The Marinade:

- 3 tbsp. sesame oil
- ½ cup of soy sauce

- 2 tbsp. lemon juice
- ½ cup of orange juice
- 2 tbsp. Chopped fresh parsley
- ½ tsp. oregano
- 1 tbsp. minced garlic
- 2 tbsp. brown sugar
- 1 tsp. Kosher salt
- ½ tsp. pepper

The Glaze:

- 2 tbsp. maple syrup
- 1 tbsp. balsamic vinegar

The Heat:

- Mesquite wood pellets

Directions:

1. Combine sesame oil with soy sauce, lemon juice, and orange juice, then mix well.

2. Add oregano, minced garlic, brown sugar, kosher salt, pepper, chopped parsley to the wet mixture, and then stir until incorporated.

3. Carefully apply the wet mixture over the tuna fillet and marinate it for 2 hours. Store it in the refrigerator to keep the tuna fresh.

4. After 2 hours, remove the marinated tuna from the wood pellet smoker and thaw it at room temperature.

5. Plug the wood pellet smoker and place the wood pellet inside the hopper. Turn the switch on.

6. Set the temperature to 225°F (107°C) and prepare the wood pellet smoker for indirect heat. Wait until the wood pellet smoker is ready.

7. Place the marinated tuna fillet in the wood pellet smoker and smoke it until flaky.

8. Once it is done, remove the smoked tuna fillet from the wood pellet smoker and transfer it to a serving dish.

9. Mix the maple syrup with balsamic vinegar, then baste the mixture over the smoked tuna fillet.

10. Serve and enjoy.

Nutrition:

- Amount per 195 g
- = 1 serving(s)
- Energy (calories): 206 kcal
- Protein: 35.84 g
- Fat: 4.96 g
- Carbohydrates: 4.98 g

49. Smoked Trout with Fennel & Black Pepper Rub

Preparation time: 15 minutes

Cooking time: 2 hours 10 minutes

Servings: 10

Ingredients:

- Trout fillet (4,5-lb., 2.3-kg.)

The Rub:

- 2 tbsp. lemon juice
- 3 tbsp. fennel seeds
- 1 ½ tbsp. ground coriander
- 1 tbsp. Black pepper
- ½ tsp. chili powder
- 1 tsp. kosher salt
- 1 tsp. garlic powder

The Glaze:

- 3 tbsp. olive oil

The Heat:

- Mesquite wood pellets

Directions:

1. Drizzle lemon juice over the trout fillet and let it rest for approximately 10 minutes.
2. In the meantime, combine the fennel seeds with coriander, black pepper, chili powder, salt, and garlic powder, then mix well.
3. Rub the trout fillet with the spice mixture, then set aside.
4. Plug the wood pellet smoker and place the wood pellet inside the hopper. Turn the switch on.
5. Set the temperature to 225°F (107°C) and prepare the wood pellet smoker for indirect heat. Wait until the wood pellet smoker is ready.
6. Place the seasoned trout fillet in the wood pellet smoker and smoke it for 2 hours.
7. Baste olive oil over the trout fillet and repeat it once every 20 minutes.

8. Once the smoked trout flakes, remove it from the wood pellet smoker and transfer it to a serving dish.

9. Serve and enjoy.

Nutrition:

- Energy (calories): 185 kcal
- Protein: 47.32 g
- Fat: 17.18 g
- Carbohydrates: 0.94 g

50. Sweet Smoked Shrimps Garlic Butter

Preparation time: 15 minutes

Cooking time: 20 minutes

Servings: 10

Ingredients:

- Fresh shrimps (2-lbs., 0.9-kg.)

The Rub:

- 2 tbsp. Lemon juice
- ½ tsp. Salt

- ½ tsp. Black pepper

The Glaze:

- 2 tbsp. Butter
- ½ tsp. Garlic powder

The Heat:

- Hickory wood pellets

Directions:

1. Peel the fresh shrimps and drizzle lemon juice over them. Let them rest for several minutes.
2. After that, sprinkle salt and black pepper over the shrimps and spread them in a disposable aluminum pan.
3. Plug the wood pellet smoker and place the wood pellet inside the hopper. Turn the switch on.
4. Set the temperature to 200°F (93°C) and prepare the wood pellet smoker for indirect heat. Wait until the wood pellet smoker is ready.
5. Insert the aluminum pan with shrimps into the wood pellet smoker and smoke the shrimps for approximately 20 minutes.
6. Regularly check the shrimps and once they turn pink, take them out of the wood pellet smoker.
7. Add garlic powder to the butter, then mix until combined. The butter will be soft.
8. Baste the garlic butter over the smoked shrimps and serve.
9. Enjoy!

Nutrition:

- Amount per 94 g
- = 1 serving(s)
- Energy (calories): 99 kcal
- Protein: 18.6 g
- Fat: 2.01 g

- Carbohydrates: 0.21 g

51. Spiced Smoked Crabs with Lemon Grass

Preparation time: 15 minutes

Cooking time: 20 minutes

Servings: 10

Ingredients:

- Fresh crabs (5-lb., 2.3-kg.)

The Rub:

- 2 tbsp. smoked paprika
- 1 tsp. kosher salt
- 2 tbsp. dried parsley
- 2 tbsp. dried thyme
- 1 tbsp. black pepper
- 1 tsp. cayenne pepper
- 1 tsp. Allspice
- ½ tsp. Ground ginger
- ½ tsp. cinnamon powder
- Two lemongrass

The Heat:

- Hickory wood pellets

Directions:

1. Combine the smoked paprika, salt, parsley, thyme, black pepper, ground ginger, cinnamon powder, cayenne pepper, and allspice, then mix well.
2. Arrange the crabs in a disposable aluminum pan, then sprinkle the spice mixture over them.
3. Add lemongrasses on top, then cover the seasoned crabs with aluminum foil.
4. Plug the wood pellet smoker and place the wood pellet inside the hopper. Turn the switch on.
5. Set the temperature to 200°F (93°C) and prepare the wood pellet smoker for indirect heat. Wait until the wood pellet smoker is ready.
6. Insert the aluminum pan with crabs into the wood pellet smoker and smoke the crabs for 30 minutes.
7. Once it is done, take the smoked crabs out of the wood pellet smoker and serve.
8. Enjoy!

Nutrition:

- Amount per 229 g
- = 1 serving(s)
- Energy (calories): 201 kcal
- Protein: 41.14 g
- Fat: 2.58 g
- Carbohydrates: 0.98 g

52. Tequila Orange Marinade Smoked Lobster

Preparation time: 15 minutes

Cooking time: 1 hour 10 minutes

Servings: 10

Ingredients:

- Fresh lobsters (5-lb., 2.3-kg.)

The Marinade:

- ¼ cup Tequila
- 3 tbsp. Lemon juice
- Two cups Orange juice
- ½ tsp. Grated lemon zest
- ½ tsp. Grated orange zest
- 1 tsp. Kosher salt
- ¼ tsp. Pepper

The Heat:

- Hickory wood pellets

Directions:

1. Mix the tequila with lemon juice and orange juice, then stir well.

2. Add grated lemon zest, orange zest, salt, and pepper to the liquid mixture, then stir until dissolved.

3. Drizzle the mixture over the lobsters and marinate them for at least 2 hours. Store the marinated lobsters in the refrigerator to keep them fresh.

4. After 2 hours, take the marinated lobsters out of the refrigerator and thaw them at room temperature.

5. Plug the wood pellet smoker and place the wood pellet inside the hopper. Turn the switch on.

6. Set the temperature to 200°F (93°C) and prepare the wood pellet smoker for indirect heat. Wait until the wood pellet smoker is ready.

7. Arrange the marinated lobsters in the wood pellet smoker and smoke them for an hour or until the smoked lobsters' internal temperature reaches 145°F (63°C).

8. Remove the smoked lobsters from the wood pellet smoker and transfer them to a serving dish.

9. Serve and enjoy.

Nutrition:

- Amount per 192 g
- = 1 serving(s)
- Energy (calories): 189 kcal
- Protein: 37.66 g
- Fat: 1.74 g
- Carbohydrates: 3.42 g

53. Beer Butter Smoked Clams

Preparation time: 15 minutes

Cooking time: 30 minutes

Servings: 10

Ingredients:

- Fresh clams (5-lb., 2.3-kg.)

The Sauce:

- One bottle beer
- 2 tbsp. olive oil
- 2 tbsp. minced garlic
- 1 tsp. salt
- ¼ cup butter

The Heat:

- Hickory wood pellets

Directions:

1. Preheat a saucepan over medium heat, then pour olive oil into it.

2. Once the oil is hot, stir in the minced garlic and sauté until wilted and aromatic.

3. Remove the saucepan from heat, then pour beer into it.

4. Add salt to the mixture, then stir until incorporated.

5. Spread the clams in a disposable aluminum pan, then pour the beer mixture over the clams.

6. Drop butter at several places on top of the clams, then set aside.

7. Plug the wood pellet smoker and place the wood pellet inside the hopper. Turn the switch on.

8. Set the temperature to 200°F (93°C) and prepare the wood pellet smoker for indirect heat. Wait until the wood pellet smoker is ready.

9. Insert the aluminum pan with clams into the wood pellet smoker and smoke the clams for half an hour.

10. Once it is done and the smoked clams' shells are open, take them out of the wood pellet smoker.

11. Transfer the smoked clams to a serving dish and enjoy.

Nutrition:

- Amount per 138 g
- = 1 serving(s)
- Energy (calories): 137 kcal
- Protein: 1.51 g
- Fat: 3.41 g
- Carbohydrates: 25.12 g

54. Chile Lime Clams with Tomatoes and Grilled Bread

Preparation time: 10 minutes

Cooking time: 25 minutes

Servings: 4

Ingredients:

- 6 tbsp unsalted pieces of butter
- Two large shallots, chopped
- Four thinly sliced garlic cloves
- 1 tbsp of tomato paste
- 1 cup of beer
- 1 cup cherry tomatoes
- 1 1/2 ounce can-chickpeas, rinsed
- 2 tbsp sambal oelek
- 24 scrubbed littleneck clams
- 1 tbsp fresh lime juice
- Four thick slices of country-style bread
- 2 tbsp olive oil
- Kosher salt
- ½ cup cilantro leaves
- lime wedges

Intolerances:

- Gluten-Free
- Egg-Free

Directions:

1. Set up the grill for medium, indirect heat. Put a large skillet on the grill over direct heat and melt 4 tbsp of butter in it.
2. Add the shallots and garlic and keep cooking, often stirring, until they soften about 4 minutes.
3. Add the tomato paste and keep cooking, continually stirring, until paste darkens to a rich brick red color. Add the beer and tomatoes.
4. Cook until the beer is reduced nearly by half, about 4 minutes. Add in the chickpeas and sambal oelek, then the clams.
5. Cover and keep cooking until clams have opened, maybe from 5 to 10 minutes, depending on the size of clams and the heat. Discard any clams that don't open. Pour in the lime juice and the remaining 2 tbsp of butter.
6. While grilling the clams, you can sprinkle the bread with oil and season with salt. Grill until it becomes golden brown and crisp.
7. Put the toasts onto plates and spoon with clam mixture, then top with cilantro. Serve with lime wedges.

Nutrition:

- Calories: 400
- Fat: 21g
- Carbs: 33g
- Protein: 17g

55. Grilled Scallops with Lemony Salsa Verde

Preparation time:

Cooking time:

Servings:

Ingredients:

- 2 tbsp of vegetable oil and more for the grill
- 12 large sea scallops, side muscle removed
- Kosher salt and ground black pepper
- Lemony Salsa Verde

Intolerances:

- Gluten-Free - Egg-Free - Lactose-Free

Directions:

1. Set up the grill for medium-high heat, then oil the grate. Toss the scallops with 2 tbsp of oil on a rimmed baking sheet and season with salt and pepper.
2. Utilizing a fish spatula or your hands, place the scallops on the grill.
3. Grill them, occasionally turning, until gently seared and cooked through, around 2 minutes for each side.
4. Serve the scallops with Lemony Salsa Verde.

Nutrition:

- Calories: 30 Fat: 1g Cholesterol: 17mg Carbs: 1g Protein: 6g

56. Blackened Salmon

Cook Time: 10 mins

Prep Time: 15 mins

Ingredients

- One tablespoon, optional cayenne pepper

- Two cloves garlic, minced

- Two tablespoons olive oil

- Four tablespoons pit boss sweet rib rub

- 2-pound salmon, fillet, scaled and deboned

Directions:

- Startup your Pit Boss Grill. Once it's fired up, set the temperature to 350°F.

- Remove the skin from the salmon and discard. Brush the salmon on both sides with olive oil, then rub the salmon fillet with the minced garlic, cayenne pepper, and Sweet Rib Rub.

- Grill the salmon for 5 minutes on one side. Flip the salmon and then grill for another 5 minutes, or until the salmon reaches an internal temperature of 145°F. Remove from the grill and serve.

57. Lemon Smoked Salmon

Cook Time: 60 Mins

Prep Time: 5 Mins

Ingredients

- Dill, fresh

- 1 lemon, sliced

- 1 1/2 - 2 lbs salmon, fresh

Directions:

- Preheat your grill to 225°F.

- Place the salmon on a cedar plank. Lay the lemon slices along the top of the salmon. Smoke in your Grill for about 60 minutes.

- Top with fresh dill and serve.

58. Grilled Lobster Tails

Cook Time: 10 Mins

Prep Time: 10 Mins

Ingredients

- Tt black pepper

- 3/4 stick butter, room temp

- Two tablespoons chives, chopped

- One clove garlic, minced

- Lemon, sliced

- 3 (7-ounce) lobster, tail

- Tt salt, kosher

Directions:

- Start your grill on "SMOKE" with the lid open until a fire is established in the burn pot (3-7 minutes).

- Preheat grill to 350°F.

- Blend butter, chives, minced garlic, and black pepper in a small bowl. Cover with plastic wrap and set aside.

- Butterfly the tails down the middle of the softer underside of the shell. Don't cut entirely through the center of the meat. Brush the tails with olive oil and season with salt to your liking.

- Grill lobsters cut side down about 5 minutes until the shells are bright red. Flip the tails over and top with a generous tablespoon of herb butter. Grill for another 4 minutes, or until the lobster meat is an opaque white color.

- Remove from the grill and serve with more herb butter and lemon wedges.

59. Grilled Oysters

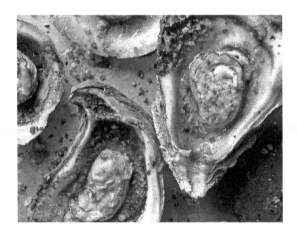

Prep Time: 20 Minutes

Cook Time: 30 Minutes

Pellets: Hickory

Nail National Oyster Day with this recipe from Journey South. Start with a sautéed mixture of onion, bell peppers, garlic, and lemon juice. Add in some Pit Boss Chicken Rub and white wine and let this sauce make those oysters sing.

How Many People Are You Serving? 4

Ingredients

- 2 Medium onion

- 1 Medium Bell Pepper, Red

- 5 Tablespoon extra-virgin olive oil

- 2 lemons

- 3 teaspoon dried thyme

- 3 dried bay leaves

- 5 Tablespoon garlic, minced

- 3 Tablespoon Pit Boss Chicken Rub

- 3 Tablespoon Worcestershire sauce

- 5 Tablespoon Hot Pepper Sauce

- 1/4 cup white wine

- 4 Butter, Sticks

- 12 Whole Oysters, shucked

- As Needed Italian Cheese Blend

Steps

1. When ready to cook, set grill temperature to High and preheat, lid closed for 15 minutes.

2. Preheat olive oil in a cast-iron pan over medium heat. Chop onion and bell peppers and place in preheated pan.

3. Juice lemons into sauté pan. Add thyme, bay leaves, garlic, and mix in the Pit Boss Chicken Rub.

4. Sauté the vegetable mixture until onions are translucent and peppers have softened about 5-7 minutes.

5. Add the Worcestershire Sauce and hot sauce. Add white wine and 4 sticks of butter. Sauté for another 15 minutes.

6. While the sauce is simmering, clean and shuck the oysters leaving them at the bottom of the shell.

7. Place oysters on Pit Boss and top with the sauce. Cook for 5 minutes.

8. Top with Italian cheese and serve. Enjoy!

60. Smoked Trout

Prep Time: 10 Minutes

Cook Time: 2 Hours

Pellets: Oak

This easy smoked trout recipe allows the fish and smoke flavors to shine on their own. Simply butterfly the trout, brine for an hour, let it smoke then serve it up hot or cold.

How Many People Are You Serving? 6

Ingredients

- 8 rainbow trout fillets

- 1 Gallon water

- 1/4 cup salt

- 1/2 cup brown sugar

- 1 Tablespoon black pepper

- 2 Tablespoon soy sauce

Steps

1. Clean the fresh fish and butterfly them.

2. For the Brine: Combine one-gallon water, brown sugar, soy sauce, salt, and pepper and stir until salt and sugar are dissolved. Brine the trout in the refrigerator for 60 minutes.

3. When ready to cook, set Pit Boss temperature to 225°F and preheat, lid closed for 15 minutes. For optimal flavor, use Super Smoke if available. Grill: 225°

4. Remove the fish from the brine and pat dry. Place fish directly on the grill grate for 1-1/2 to 2 hours, depending on the thickness of the trout. Fish is done when it turns opaque and starts to flake. Serve hot or cold. Grill: 225°

5. Fish is done when it turns opaque and starts to flake. Serve hot or cold. Enjoy!

61. Sweet Mandarin Salmon

Prep Time: 5 Minutes

Cook Time: 10 Minutes

Pellets: Alder

Our sweet mandarin salmon recipe features tangy Pit Boss Mandarin Glaze with a hint of fresh lime juice and seasonings. Brush it onto a salmon filet and finish it on the Pit Boss for flaky seafood perfection.

How Many People Are You Serving? 2

Ingredients

- 1 Whole lime juice

- 1 teaspoon sesame oil

- 1 Jar Pit Boss Mandarin Glaze

- 3/2 Tablespoon soy sauce

- 2 Tablespoon cilantro, finely chopped

- To Taste cracked black pepper

- 1 Pinch Jacobsen Salt Co. Pure Kosher Sea Salt

- 1 Whole Salmon, cut into fillets

Steps

1. Start your Pit Boss on High for 10 to 15 minutes, lid closed.

2. For the glaze, combine Mandarin Glaze, lime juice, sesame oil, soy sauce, cilantro, and fresh cracked black pepper. Mix.

3. Cut the salmon into 4 fillets. Brush with glaze and place directly on the grill grate, skin side down.

4. Cook until salmon reaches an internal temperature of 155 degrees F (about 15-20 minutes). Halfway through cook time, brush salmon again with the glaze.

5. Remove the salmon from the grill and serve with the remaining glaze if desired. Enjoy!

Vegetable Recipes

62. Grilled Whole Chicken

Prep time: 5 minutes | Cook time: 1 hour 10 minutes | Serves 4

1 (4 pounds) whole chicken, giblets removed

Traeger Chicken Rub, as needed

1. When ready to cook, set Traeger temperature to 375°F (191°C) and preheat, lid closed for 15 minutes.

2. Rinse and pat dry the chicken. Season the whole chicken lightly, including the cavity, with Traeger Chicken Rub.

3. Arrange the chicken on the grill and cook for about 1 hour and 10 minutes, or until the internal temperature of the chicken registers 160°F (71°C).

4. Remove the chicken from the grill and set aside to rest for 15 to 20 minutes, or until it has an internal temperature of 165°F (74°C). Serve warm.

63. Brine Smoked Chicken

Prep time: 10 minutes | Cook time: 3 hours | Serves 6

1 cup brown sugar

½ cup kosher salt

1 (3 to 3½ pounds / 1.4 to 1.6 kg) whole chicken

One teaspoon minced garlic

Traeger Big Game Rub, as needed

One medium yellow onion, quartered

One lemon halved

Three whole garlic clove

Five thyme sprigs

1. Make the Brine: Dissolve the kosher salt and brown sugar in 1 gallon of water. Once dissolved, put the chicken into the brine, ensuring the chicken is completely submerged, then place in the refrigerator overnight.

2. When ready to cook, set Traeger temperature to 225°F (107°C) and preheat, lid closed for 15 minutes. For optimal flavor, use Super Smoke if available.

3. Remove the chicken from the brine and pat dry with paper towels. Rub the minced garlic and Traeger Big Game Rub over the chicken. Stuff the cavity with the onion, lemon, garlic clove, and thyme sprigs. Tie the legs together.

4. Arrange the chicken on the grill and smoke for 2½ to 3 hours or until an instant-read thermometer reads 160°F (71°C) when inserted into the thickest part of the chicken.

5. Remove the chicken from the grill and let rest for 15 minutes before serving (the internal temperature will rise to 165°F (74°C) as the chicken rests).

64. Roasted Christmas Goose

Prep time: 30 minutes | Cook time: 2 hours | Serves 8

5½ pounds (2.5 kg) goose

Two limes, zested and cut into wedges

Two lemons, zested and cut into wedges

Two teaspoons salt, plus more as needed

Two thyme sprigs

Two sage sprigs

One medium green apple, cut into wedges

Three tablespoons honey

1. When ready to cook, set Traeger temperature to High and preheat, lid closed for 15 minutes.

2. Using the tip of a sharp knife, lightly score the breast and leg skin in a criss-cross pattern. Combine the citrus zest with the salt in a bowl. Generously season the cavity of the goose with salt, then rub the citrus mix well into the skin and sprinkle some inside the cavity. Stuff the goose with thyme, sage, lime, lemon, and apple wedges.

3. Arrange the stuffed goose on the grill cook for 40 minutes.

4. Brush the honey on top of the goose and reduce the temperature to 325°F (163°C). Continue to cook for 1½ to 2 hours, or until an instant-read thermometer inserted in the thickest part of the goose registers 160°F (71°C).

5. Remove the goose from the grill and lightly tent with foil. Let rest in the foil for 30 minutes before serving.

Prep time: 15 minutes | Cook time: 1 hour 10 minutes | Serves 9

Two whole chicken, giblets removed

Six clove garlic, minced

Two tablespoons salt

Three tablespoons pimentón, plus additional for sprinkling

Six tablespoons extra-virgin olive oil, divided

Two bunch fresh thyme

3 pounds (1.4 kg) Yukon gold potatoes, scrubbed

Salt and ground black pepper, to taste

Two lemons halved

½ cup chopped flat-leaf parsley

1. Rinse the chickens, inside and out, under cold running water. Pat them dry with paper towels. Tie the legs together with butcher's string and tuck the wings behind the backs.

2. Stir together the minced garlic, pimentón, and salt in a small bowl. Whisk in 3 tablespoons of olive oil. Slather the mixture all over the outside of the chickens. Tuck one bunch of thyme inside the main cavity of each chicken. Arrange the chickens on a rimmed baking sheet and transfer them to the refrigerator, uncovered, for at least 6 hours or overnight.

3. In a large bowl, toss the potatoes with salt, pepper, and the remaining three tablespoons of olive oil. Spread the potatoes in a large roasting pan.

4. Place the chickens side by side on top of the potatoes. Squeeze the lemons over the chickens and add the rinds to the potatoes.

5. When ready to cook, set Traeger temperature to 400°F (204°C) and preheat, lid closed for 10 to 15 minutes.

6. Place the roasting pan with the chickens and potatoes on the grill and roast for 30 minutes. Stir the potatoes.

7. Reduce the temperature to 350°F (177°C) and continue to roast for about 40 minutes, or until an instant-read meat thermometer inserted into the thickest part of the thighs registers 165°F (74°C).

8. Transfer the potatoes and lemons to a large platter. Lightly sprinkle additional pimentón on top and garnish with the parsley. Place the chickens on top and serve.

66. Cajun Wings

Prep time: 15 minutes | Cook time: 30 minutes | Serves 4

2 pounds (907 g) chicken wings

Traeger Cajun Shake, as needed

Traeger Pork & Poultry Rub, as needed

1. In a large bowl, toss the chicken wings with Traeger Cajun Shake and Traeger Pork & Poultry Rub.

2. When ready to cook, set the Traeger to 350°F (177°C) and preheat, lid closed for 15 minutes.

3. Lay the chicken wings on the grill and cook for 30 minutes, or until the skin is browned and the center is juicy, and an instant-read thermometer reaches at least 165°F (74°C).

4. Let rest for 5 minutes before serving.

67. Spicy Chicken Skewers

Prep time: 3 hours | Cook time: 20 minutes | Serves 6

16 ounces (454 g) chicken breast, cubed

½ cup ranch

Two tablespoons chile sauce

½ teaspoon dried oregano

½ teaspoon garlic powder

One whole red onion, sliced

One whole green bell peppers, sliced

Eight strips bacon, sliced

1. Toss the chicken breast with the ranch, chile sauce, oregano, and garlic powder in a large bowl until evenly coated. Marinate for 1 to 3 hours in the refrigerator.

2. When ready to cook, set Traeger temperature to High and preheat, lid closed for 15 minutes.

3. Assemble the Traeger skewers: Slide on a slice of onion, a slice of bell pepper, a slice of bacon, and chicken. Continue to alternate the bacon and chicken, so the bacon weaves around the chicken pieces. Finish off each skewer with a slice of bell pepper and onion. Be sure not to overcrowd skewer and repeat with all skewers.

4. Arrange the skewers on the grill, keeping a piece of foil under the end of the skewers to prevent them from burning and to make turning them easier. Grill each side for approximately 5 minutes, doing a quarter-turn each time, for a total of 20 minutes, or until the chicken reads an internal temperature of 165°F (74°C).

5. Remove the skewers from the grill and serve hot.

68. Tandoori Chicken Wings

Prep time: 30 minutes | Cook time: 50 minutes | Serves 4

Marinade:

¼ cup yogurt

One tablespoon minced cilantro leaves

One whole scallion, minced

Two teaspoons ginger, minced

One teaspoon garam masala

One teaspoon ground black pepper

One teaspoon salt

Wings:

1½ pounds (680 g) chicken wings

Cooking spray

Sauce:

¼ cup yogurt

Two tablespoons cucumber

Two tablespoons mayonnaise

Two teaspoons lemon juice

½ teaspoon salt

½ teaspoon cumin

⅛ teaspoon cayenne pepper

1. Place the yogurt, cilantro, scallions, ginger, garam masala, pepper, and salt in a blender and pulse until smooth.

2. Place the chicken wings in a large resealable plastic bag and pour the yogurt mixture over the chicken wings, massaging the bag to coat all the wings. Let marinate for 4 to 8 hours in the refrigerator.

3. Drain the chicken wings of excess marinade, discarding the marinade.

4. When ready to cook, set Traeger temperature to 350°F (177°C) and preheat, lid closed for 10 to 15 minutes. Oil the grill grates with cooking spray.

5. Lay the chicken wings on the grill and cook for 45 to 50 minutes until the skin is crispy, flipping the wings once or twice during cooking.

6. Meanwhile, whisk all the sauce ingredients to combine in a bowl and refrigerate until ready to use.

7. When the wings are done, transfer them to a platter and serve alongside the prepared sauce.

69. Pan-Roasted Game Birds

Prep time: 10 minutes | Cook time: 1 hour | Serves 6

4 pounds (1.8 kg) game birds

Four tablespoons melted butter, divided

Salt and black pepper, to taste

Two whole lemons halved

One bunch of fresh thyme

One bunch of fresh parsley

One bunch of fresh rosemary

1. When ready to cook, set Traeger temperature to high and preheat, lid closed for 15 minutes. Put a large cast-iron skillet on the grill while preheating.

2. Rub two tablespoons of butter all over the game birds and season the inside and outside with salt and pepper.

3. Stuff the cavity of each bird with half a lemon, a sprig of parsley, thyme, and rosemary. Truss the birds by simply tying the legs together with string.

4. Add the remaining two tablespoons of butter to the cast iron skillet on the grill. Place the birds in the hot cast iron skillet and roast for 45 to 60 minutes or until the internal temperature reaches 165°F (74°C).

5. Rest for 10 minutes before serving.

70. Glazed Chicken Breasts

Prep time: 20 minutes | Cook time: 30 minutes | Serves 4

¼ cup olive oil

One tablespoon Worcestershire sauce

One teaspoon freshly pressed garlic

Traeger Fin & Feather Rub, as needed

Four whole chicken breasts

½ cup Traeger 'Que BBQ sauce

½ cup Traeger Sweet & Heat BBQ Sauce

1. Whisk together the olive oil, Worcestershire sauce, garlic, and Traeger Fin & Feather rub in a small bowl. Rub the mixture all over the chicken breasts. Combine both sauces in another bowl and set aside.

2. When ready to cook, set Traeger temperature to 500°F (260°C) and preheat, lid closed for 15 minutes.

3. Arrange the chicken breasts on the grill and cook for 20 to 30 minutes or until the internal temperature reaches 160°F (71°C) when inserted into the thickest part of the breasts. Glaze the chicken breasts with the sauce mixture during the last 5 minutes of cooking.

4. Remove the chicken breasts from the grill and cool for 5 minutes before serving.

71. Roasted Tomatoes

Prep Time: 5 Minutes

Cook Time : 3 Hours

Pellets: Alder

For a perfectly balanced meal, accompany your main meat event with this delicious, colorful, & healthy side dish.

How Many People Are You Serving? 2

Ingredients

- 3 large ripe tomatoes

- 1/2 Tablespoon kosher salt

- 1 teaspoon coarse ground black pepper

- 1/4 teaspoon sugar

- 1/4 Teaspoon thyme or basil

- As Needed olive oil

Steps

1. Line a rimmed baking sheet with parchment paper.

2. When ready to cook, set Pit Boss temperature to 225°F and preheat, lid closed for 15 minutes.

Grill: 225°

3. Remove the stem end from each tomato and cut the tomatoes into 1/2 inch thick slices.

4. Combine the salt, pepper, sugar, and thyme or basil in a small bowl and mix.

5. Pour olive oil into the well of a dinner plate.

6. Dip one side of each tomato slice in the olive oil and arrange on the baking sheet. Dust the tomato slices with the seasoning mixture.

7. Arrange the pan directly on the grill grate and roast the tomatoes until the juices stop running and the edges have contracted about 3 hours. Remove from grill and enjoy it!

Prep Time: 30 Minutes

Cook Time: 10 Minutes

Pellets: Cherry

This grilled fruit recipe is a sure-fire way to impress every last guest at your neighborhood BBQ.

How Many People Are You Serving? 4

Ingredients

- 8 Slices seedless watermelon

- To Taste sea salt

- 2 Tablespoon honey

Steps

1. Lightly sprinkle the watermelon wedges on both sides with salt.

2. Stand the watermelon wedges on their edges on a rack over a sink or pan and let them drain for half an hour.

3. When ready to cook, set Pit Boss temperature to 500°F and preheat, lid closed for 15 minutes. Grill: 500°

4. After the watermelon has drained, rinse each piece under cold running water. Place each piece between two folded paper towels and gently but firmly press to remove excess water.

5. Brush the watermelon lightly on both sides with the honey.

6. Place the watermelon slices on the grill grate and Pit Boss them until grill marks have formed and the melon is slightly softened about 5 minutes. Grill: 500°

7. Remove from grill and sprinkle with sea salt and squeeze fresh lime juice over the top. Enjoy!

VEGETARIAN RECIPES

Prep Time: 10 Minutes

Cook Time: 30 Minutes

Pellets: Mesquite

Who knew smoked tomatoes would be so amazing? Chef Timothy did. Pair it with just about anything. Hell, put it on cardboard and you'll have a winner. It's that good.

How Many People Are You Serving? 4

Ingredients

- 3 cup diced Roma tomatoes

- 1 jalapeño, diced

- 1/2 red onion, diced

- 1/2 bunch cilantro, finely chopped

- 2 lime, juiced

- To Taste salt

- To Taste olive oil

Steps

1. When ready to cook, set Pit Boss temperature to 180°F and preheat, lid closed for 15 minutes. For optimal flavor, use Super Smoke if available. Grill: 180°

2. Place the diced tomatoes on a small sheet pan spreading them into a thin layer. Place the sheet pan directly on the grill and smoke for 30 minutes. Grill: 180°

3. When the tomatoes are finished, toss all ingredients in a medium bowl and finish with lime juice, salt, and olive oil to taste. Serve and enjoy!

74. Grilled Winter Chop Salad

Prep Time : 20 Minutes

Cook Time : 10 Minutes

Pellets : Hickory

Grilled radicchio and endive lettuce, toasted almonds, salami, and provolone cheese combined with a grilled lemon vinaigrette for a colorfully fresh chopped winter salad.

How Many People Are You Serving? 4

Ingredients

- 2 Head radicchio, quartered

- 2 Head endive, chopped

- 2 Head endive, chopped

- As Needed olive oil

- As Needed kosher salt

- As Needed freshly ground black pepper

- 2 Whole lemons, halved

- 1/2 coarsely chopped almonds

- 1 Small shallot, finely diced

- 1/4 Cup red wine vinegar

- 1 Teaspoon salt

- 1/2 Cup olive oil

- 1/2 Teaspoon freshly ground black pepper

- 1 (5-1/2 oz) log salami, diced into 1/2 inch pieces

- 1/2 Cup diced provolone cheese

- 4 Whole fire-roasted red peppers, drained and cut into thin strips

- 1 pear or apple, diced into 1/2 inch pieces

Steps

1. When ready to cook, set Pit Boss temperature to 375°F and preheat, lid closed for 15 minutes. Grill: 375°

2. Drizzle the radicchio and endive with olive oil and season with salt and pepper.

3. When the grill is up to temperature, add the lettuces and cook with the lid closed for 2 to 4 minutes per side, until they begin to wilt. Remove from the grill. Grill: 375°

4. Drizzle halved lemons with olive oil and place cut-side down on the grill for 2 to 3 minutes. Grill: 375°

5. In an oven-proof skillet, add the almonds to the grill. Close the lid and toast for 2 to 3 minutes. Remove from the grill. Grill: 375°

6. To Make the Vinaigrette: Combine shallots, red wine vinegar, and the grilled lemon juice in a bowl and add salt. While whisking the red wine vinegar mixture, slowly pour in olive oil until combined. Add black pepper.

7. Chop the grilled lettuces into bite-sized pieces and arrange in a bowl. Top with endive, salami, provolone, peppers, pears, and toasted almonds. Toss with vinaigrette and season with salt and pepper to taste. Enjoy!

Introduction

Barbeque is a huge part of American cuisine and culture. Smoked meats are a favorite among the entire country. Barbeque becomes a must in summers when families get together on long summer weekends, spending quality time together. Nowadays, this has become nearly impossible because of the tough work-life balance and people's desire to grab an easy bite. No one has the time and energy to set up the conventional-style barbeque. Some people might still be up for doing all the hard work, but most of the population would welcome a quick and easy way to enjoy the smoked flavors of barbequed meat.

Technology has made this difficult feat possible. Electric Smokers are a great appliance that makes our job simple. There was a time when you had to spend the whole day in front of the Smoker to prepare a good smoked steak. With the electric Smoker, you can enjoy the authentic flavor of barbeque with little effort. What the electric Smoker does is that it uses the same conventional method for cooking, but you do not have to do all the hard work manually; the electric Smoker does it for you. All you must do is prepare the meat, set up the electric Smoker, pour in some water in the water tray, throw in some wood chips, turn up the heat according to your needs and set the timer.

Meanwhile, you go about your business, run your errands, have a chat with your friends, and your yummy food is being prepared all on its own. You do not need to worry about temperature control or about managing the charcoal. The electric Smoker fits best with the modern way of life. Another huge advantage of electric smokers, apart from them being super easy to operate, is that they are easy to clean. They are just like little closets which have removable racks. You can remove every part, clean it, and place it back. Also, because the temperature and the smoke can be regulated and controlled, the result is perfect most of the time. The chances for mishaps are rare, unlike the traditional style, where things can get tricky quite often.

If you want to enjoy a delicious barbeque with the least effort, you should read on about this amazing appliance, making you a pro at family barbeques in no time. Enjoy reading!

Chapter 1: What is an Electric Smoker?

In this chapter, the basic introduction and working of the electric Smoker will be discussed. Before understanding the Electric Smoker, we must first understand the meaning of the cooking method that the Electric Smoker uses.

This technique is known as 'Smoking,' and it is a type of process related to barbeque.

75. 1.1. What is Smoking?

Smoking is a more specialized and extreme type of barbecuing. You will be using the smoke from different types of aromatic wood chips or wood chunks in smoking. You may use wood chips of cherry, apple, hickory, mesquite, and many others. These impart their unique flavor and smoky aroma to the meat being smoked.

The process of smoking takes longer than barbecuing. The temperature is also lower than barbecue. The temperature is usually set between 125 to 175°F. The temperature is kept lower because if the temperature is turned up, then the meat's outer layer will be cooked and will not allow the smoke to reach throughout the meat and impart its rich aroma and taste.

Smoking is an advanced technique, and it required a much longer time for food preparation than grilling and normal barbeque. This method also requires a maximum amount of expertise to understand the texture of different types of meat and how they will be perfectly smoked.

1.2   The Electric Smoker

An electric smoker is a cooking appliance that is used outside. Smoking is an advanced type of variation of barbecue. The electric Smoker uses an electric source and heating rods to produce heat for cooking and smoking. The conventional way to smoke is to burn charcoal to produce the required heat, but the electric Smoker is easier to use and simple to operate. The whole process is cleaner as compared to the conventional style. The body of the electric Smoker is either made of stainless steel or cast iron.

(An electric smoker)

There are numerous different types of electric smokers available in the market. You have an option to choose a smoker that is according to your requirements. Different models vary in their specific features, size, number of cooking racks present, temperature control features, number of cycles, preheat options, keep warm option, manual settings, automatic settings, digital displays, and control panels.

Sometimes variety can also overwhelm a buyer. To buy an electric smoker, it is recommended to first determine your requirements and then research the market too but the proper kind of Smoker for yourself. In the following pages, you will also find guidelines to help you decide whether you even need an electric smoker or not. Before that, we will briefly discuss the common features present in almost all electric smokers.

1.3 Working of an Electric Smoker

Normally, when you see an electric smoker, it looks like a cabinet; it is quite efficient in smoking the meat with relatively few components. The basic heating function is that the electric rods heat the entire cooking chamber, and the heated air is spread throughout the chamber. This causes the meat to cook by convection. There are six basic components of the electric Smoker:

- Cooking Chamber
- Woodchip tray
- Electric Heating rods or other heating elements
- Racks or grills to place the meat.
- Water Pan

1.3.1 Cooking Chamber

Like the gas smokers and the charcoal smokers, the electric smokers also have a vertical alignment. The space designated for cooking is at the top. The electric heating rods are placed at the bottom of the cooking chamber. Above the heating, rods are the grills, wood chips drawer and the water pan.

1.3.2 Electric Heating Rods:

The electric rods are placed at the base of the electric Smoker. They are the main source of heat for cooking. Some models of the electric Smoker have one heating rod, and some have more than one rods. This depends on the shape and size of the electric Smoker.

1.3.3 Wood Chip Tray

This is a specific space or tray provided above the electric rods to place the wood chips or wood chunks within the heating chamber. When the woodchips burn slowly, they cause smoke, which spreads within the cooking chamber and surrounds the meat. This smoke gives the meat a smoky and rich flavor. The woodchip tray is sometimes called the firebox as well.

Different types of hardwood are available to put in the electric Smoker. You can use various wood chips and chunks of mesquite, oak, alder, apple, cherry, maple, and hickory.

1.3.4 Water Pan

This is like a slightly deep pan or tray, fixed like a rack in the electric Smoker. Before starting the Smoker, this tray is filled with cold water. The main function is that when the heating rods are turned on, this cold water keeps the temperature from rising quickly inside the heating chamber. The other function is that steam is created when the water is heated up to a boiling point, which helps cook the meat. The steam helps the convection cooking process.

1.3.5 Grills or Racks

Above the water, the tray has placed the racks or grills. These are made of stainless steel. The food is placed on these for cooking. You can put the meat directly on the grill, or you can use heatproof skillets or barbecue utensils.

1.3.6 Vents and Dampers

the vents are usually placed at the top part of the electric Smoker. When the Smoker's temperature gets too high, the vents are opened to release some hot air and bring the temperature down.

The dampers are there for exactly the opposite reason. They are placed at the bottom part of the electric Smoker. When you open the dampers, oxygen enters the cooking chamber. The flames of the woodchips feed on this oxygen and increase the temperature inside the chamber.

Chapter 2. Why buy an Electric Smoker?

If you are someone who loves barbecue and the rich flavor of smoked meat, you might have thought about investing in an electric smoker. Even though you think about it, you are not quite sure whether you should invest in an electric smoker or not. You cannot deny that it is an expensive appliance and if you only occasionally barbecue, this appliance is not for you. Having said that, if you enjoy preparing delicious barbecue now and then, you might want to consider the electric Smoker. Using an electric smoker is easier than the conventional barbeque method, and it is much easier to clean. If you enjoy the smoky aroma and taste in each bite of meat, you might want to ditch the conventional method and adopt electric smoking. This is perfect for that tender, aromatic, and rich smoke flavor. However, you must be warned against the prejudice that surrounds electric smokers. The die-heart conventional barbecue community may argue that the electric Smoker does not give off the meat's authentic smoky flavor. You may agree or not to this argument but investing in an electric smoker would be your best bet if you are new to smoking.

In this chapter, we will discuss the top five reasons to buy an electric smoker. The five arguments in favor of the electric Smoker are:

- Perfect choice for beginners
- The cost
- The easy usage
- You can set it up where conventional barbeque grills might not be allowed.
- The option to cold smoke

76. 2.1. Perfect Choice for Beginners

Investing in an electric smoker is a safe choice for beginners. Smoking is a slightly tricky technique. If you go by the conventional way, it might take you longer to learn and maybe you might give up early on. With the electric Smoker, you can operate it with ease. The temperature and length of cooking can be regulated, and the best part is that the results are almost always perfect. Getting perfect results in cooking is a huge plus because it further motivates you.

Using the electric Smoker, you can learn and become familiar with the basic method and technique involved. Once you have learned the basics, you can either move on to the more conventional style or even decide to stick to the electric Smoker.

77. 2.2. The Cost

If you survey the market, you will find that electric smokers are cheaper than their conventional counterparts. When you look closely, the amount of food they can cook in one session is quite commendable. Another reason the electric Smoker might feel more appealing is that it needs only a one-time setup. After the initial setup, no maintenance is required. Cleaning is easy. To operate is easy. So, in the long run, this seems to be a better investment.

78. 2.3. The Easy Usage

If you see the conventional system of smoking and barbecue, you have a lot to manage. You must control the optimum temperature, need the expertise to light the charcoal, maintain airflow to keep a smooth temperature and manage any temperature spikes or accidents during the entire procedure. In short, you will be on your toes the whole time. Now, flip the situation to the electric Smoker. You prepare your food items, place them on the grills, fill in the water tray, put them in the woodchips, and turn on the heating rods. You can even set the time. It is as easy as this. In case you are hosting a few people over, you will have plenty of time to set up the area and interact with your guests.

79. 2.4. Can Carry the Electric Smoker Anywhere with Power Supply

The appliance comes in handy in two situations. Many states have a fire ban in summers, meaning you cannot set up a charcoal grill or do any cooking outside. There is a fear of forest fires due to the dry summer air. You can take out your electric Smoker and enjoy proper smoked food with friends and family in such a situation.

Another situation where the electric Smoker comes in handy is in small houses and apartments where space is an issue. In apartments, there is a prohibition on barbequing and smoke. You can easily set up your electric Smoker on your balcony and enjoy your favorite food in this situation.

80. 2.5. The Option to Cold Smoke

Sometimes you want to cold smoke some food items like cheese and bacon. It is not easily possible on conventional smokers. It would help if you bought the cold smoke attachments with an electric smoker, generally available easily with all-electric smoker models. This attachment can be used to prepare a variety of preparations like meatloaves, deserts, dried meat, and fish sausages.

Chapter 3. Proper Usage of the Electric Smoker

After you have purchased the Electric Smoker, comes to the process of setting it up. Most electric smokers are easy to install and setup. It is best to read the manual to understand the working of the specific model.

This chapter will discuss step-by-step how we should prepare our food items and the correct method and sequence to smoke our desired food product.

81. 3.1. Preparation of Meat

The meat preparation will be done the same way you would do for conventional barbecue and smoking as usual. Some people follow their family recipes passed down through generations. Some people prefer a marinade kept overnight; some perform a dry rub to season and prepare the meat. It is entirely up to you how you want to season the meat you want to prepare. The electric Smoker can smoke every kind of meat, so do not be shy and prepare your favorite meat for smoking. Be sure that the electric Smoker will prepare the same flavor and texture you expect from the traditional style smoker will give.

82. 3.2. Setting up the Electric Smoker

Few points should be kept in mind when setting up the electric Smoker. The first and most important is that this is an outdoor appliance. Please keep it in a properly ventilated space. It cannot be kept indoors. It must be set up outside. It should be set up on a flat and strong surface that can withstand high temperatures. Sometimes the appliance can heat-up up to high temperatures. Please keep it in an open space with room to move about so that the appliance is in no danger to be tripped over and become a hazard. Keep children away from the electric Smoker while operating and afterward until it cools down after one or two hours.

83. 3.3. Read the Electric Smoker Manual

Different models of Electric Smokers have a different set of instructions. The basic working of thee the Electric Smokers is the same, but there is a slight difference in how each Smoker is operated. It would help if you had a complete understanding of how your appliance is turned on and off, how to regulate temperature, when is it safe to open the appliance, what temperatures are suitable for which meat, how much time it requires for specific meats. It will help if you read up about all such details to use your Electric Smoker to its fullest.

84. 3.4. Seasoning the Electric Smoker

This is an important process. You only need to do this once when your electric Smoker is brand new. To get rid of any harmful chemicals left in the Smoker during manufacturing, this procedure is done. All manuals have detailed descriptions of the seasoning. You must follow the exact instructions of your Electric Smoker because they are model specific.

However, a common procedure followed for seasoning is that you apply any cooking oil on all the electric Smoker's inner surfaces such that the surfaces are completely coated. Now turn on the Electric Smoker and let it operate empty for 2 to 3 hours. Then let it cook, and then your appliance is ready for use.

85. 3.5. Preparing the Cooking Chamber

First, make sure that the cooking chamber is clean. Fill the water tray with water. This must be done before turning on the heat. Fill in the wood chip tray with wood chips or woodchucks that you wish to use. Usually, the wood chip compartment should be filled if the meat will be smoked for 3 to 4 hours. Next, set up the temperature and time for smoking. Always remember that the heating chamber should be preheated. Do not put the meat in the cold chamber and turn on the heat afterward. It is always recommended to put the meat in a well-heated chamber. This is a pro tip for the best results.

86. 3.6. Putting in the meat

First, let the cooking chamber reach a certain temperature, then place the meat on the grills. You will need to open the chamber, place the meat, and then close it. Take care of that you put in the meat swiftly so that less heat is lost from within the chamber during this action. Temperature and the correct amount of heat are essential for the meat to be prepared to perfection. It is also recommended not to open the chamber when the meat is being smoked. This might disrupt the smoking process and bring the temperature down. The same rule applies to smoking as the one that applies in baking. Optimum temperature is essential.

87. 3.7. The Process of Smoking

This is a slow process. It usually takes three or more hours. Only fish takes a shorter while to smoke. Otherwise, all other meats take much longer. Always take care to replenish the woodchips during the smoking process.

The smoking process will be carried out on its own, so there will be no other precaution except for keeping an eye on the wood chips.

Another thing to look out for will be the water. This water serves as the steam that gives the meats the required moisture that does not let them dry out. If the water is dried up, the meat will also become dry and difficult to chew on. So, it is always important that there is enough moisture circulation in the heating chamber. Always keep an eye out for the water tray. It should not be dry.

88. 3.8. Taking out the meat

Before taking out the meat from the heated chamber, always check if the meat is cooked properly. Every meat has an internal temperature that indicates its doneness. So before bringing the meat out, insert the thermometer to the thickest part of the meat can see that the optimum temperature has been achieved or not. If you think the meat is undercooked, keep it in the chamber for 20 more minutes and check again. If all seems well, take out the Smoker's rack and place it on the counter to let it rest and then slice your meat.

Serve the meat with traditional side dishes like coleslaw, corn on the cob or baked potatoes. With the electric Smoker, you do not need to worry about the meat not being cooked properly. With the temperature regulation, the chance for accidents is reduced significantly.

Chapter 4. Tips and Tricks to Smoke Anything

Knowing some tricks and hacks about appliances always helps in preparing perfect meals. The same is the case with an electric smoker. This chapter discusses a few tricks and tips to help you in preparing smoked meats and foods. Usually, we start learning with experience but learning from other's experiences can give you a head start. Here is a list of tried and tested tricks and tips for the usage of an Electric Smoker. These tips and tricks will help you along your journey with the electric Smoker. Read all the points carefully to get the best results.

89. 4.1. Do not Over Smoke the Food

When you first buy an electric smoker, you might be tempted to use many strong aromatic woodchips. But the reality is that you do not need an overpowering smoke flavor to make the barbecue delicious; only a mild smoky flavor will do the job. It is also true for poultry that over-smoked chicken becomes bitter and inedible. So always be careful about the amount of smoke you want for your food. In the case of smoke, the less is more saying is true.

90. 4.2. Smoke Chicken at High Temperature

Chicken is not one of those meat groups which need a lower temperature for a longer time to be perfectly cooked. The chicken cooks at a higher temperature. The rule of thumb is to take the temperature to 275∘F and smoke the chicken for around one to two hours. To check the chicken for doneness, insert a probe inside the chicken thigh and see that the internal temperature is about 165∘F. The proper cooking of chicken is important because undercooked chicken can cause harmful effects and infections to the body.

91. 4.3. Do not Soak the Wood Chips

It is common practice to soak woodchips in water before use. What happens is that when we soak the wood chips and put them in the Smoker and the smoking starts, white smoke is created. We think that this white smoke gives a smoky, rich flavor to the meat, but it is not true. This white smoke is just steam that dilutes the smoke's flavor and interferes with the temperature inside the chamber.

What you should do is that use the wood chips directly. The smoke that will be created will be thin blue smoke, which is the type of smoke that imparts a rich aromatic flavor to the smoked dishes.

92. 4.4. Season your Electric Smoker before Use

This point is more of a health concern rather than a tip or trick. Seasoning is the process performed before cooking anything in the Smoker. This is usually done to eliminate all factory residue, chemicals, and dust from inside the cavity that has been left over from the manufacturing plant.

This process also has a good effect on subsequent smoking as well. After the seasoning, a black layer of smoke is formed on the electric Smoker's inner surfaces. So, after seasoning, whatever you will smoke, the black coating will impart the smoky flavor.

93. 4.5. Preheat the Cooking Chamber

Always preheat the cooking chamber. Turn on the electric heat rods before putting in the meat and wait till the optimum temperature is reached; only then should you put in the meat. This will ensure that the meat will neither remain undercooked or overcooked.

94. 4.6. Put Poultry in Oven to Finish

Most of the electric smokers have a maximum temperature of 275∘F. This temperature is enough to cook poultry to perfection, but the desired crispy skins cannot be achieved at this temperature. So, if you want crispy skins, take out the chicken from the Smoker and place it in the oven at around 300∘F for 10 minutes. You will have yummy crispy skins.

95. 4.7. Cover the Racks and Grills with Aluminum Foil

This tip is more for cleanliness than the taste of the smoked good. It would help if you covered all your racks and trays with aluminum foil. This will protect the racks and grills, and whenever the aluminum gets dirty, it can be replaced with a fresh layer of aluminum foil.

96. 4.8. Do not use the Wood Chip Tray

In the electric Smoker, you fill the wood tray with woodchips. Often, people have experienced that they must refill the wood chip tray repeatedly, and it can be a bit inconvenient. Rather than wood chips, you can use a pellet smoker. A pellet smoker is a separately available tube that gives off thin blue smoke, which gives the aroma and amazing flavor to the smoked meats.

97. 4.9. Leave the Vent Open

It is a good idea to keep the vent of the Electric Smoker completely open. This is to prevent the accumulation of creosote. Creosote is a substance in smoke that gives a smoky flavor to the foods. This substance is good to impart a smoky flavor to the dish, but a high quantity of this substance can accumulate over the meat and gives off a bitter flavor.

98. 4.10. Control the Temperature Swings

The temperature swings are phenomena that are seen in all heating appliances using heating rods. What happens is that if you set the temperature of the appliance at 220∘F, the rod, when it reaches this temperature, will turn off; however, the temperature still keeps rising and is risen to about 240∘F and then starts coming back, it gets lower and lower about 210∘F, and then the rods turn on again, and it takes a while to get to 220∘F. you need to learn to manage this situation by keeping the temperature selection about 10∘F lower than the desired temperature. This way, the temperature swings will be controlled.

99. 4.11. Invest in a Good Thermometer

In smoking, you can often be confused if the meat is done or not. Sometimes you can be fooled but the appliance's internal thermostat. But the doneness of meat is determined by the internal temperature of the meat So, to check the internal temperature of the meat, you should have a separate thermometer. Such thermometers are commonly known as probes. You can insert the probe into the thickest part of the meat and determine the internal temperature. We must understand that the thermostat of the electric Smoker and the meat's internal temperature are different, and the doneness of the meat depends on the meat's internal temperature. Different meats have the different internal temperature that determines that they are fully cooked. Some meats are done at lower internal temperatures, such as fish and seafood. Some meats require high temperatures, like beef and lamb. Understanding this is especially important, and the first step towards this understanding is investing in a good thermometer.

100.   4.12. Keep the Meat Overnight Before Smoking

To achieve the meat's full flavors, it is always a good idea to keep the meat overnight. It does not matter if you decide to marinate, dry rub, or brine the meat; leaving it in the refrigerator overnight will cause the flavors to fully absorb in the meat, and the meat will also become tender before smoking. The meat will be cooked even if you decide not to let it stay overnight, but the results might not be as good as the meat that has been kept overnight. In smoking and barbecue, patience plays an important role. The more patient you are, the better your food will cook and taste.

101.   4.13. Do not Hurry.

Smoking is a long process. It takes time for meats to properly smoke. Whenever you decide to smoke meat, always keep in mind that you must have the patience to let the meat cook completely. Sometimes the temptation to check on our dishes can be harmful to the recipe. When you open the electric smoker door, the temperature is disrupted, and the recipe might be affected. Even opening the door for one or two minutes can even have such an effect. So, you must be patient while the Smoker is working. This is an amazing appliance, and you should trust it to work its wonder. All you must do is sit back and relax.

Chapter 5. Ultimate Electric Smoker Recipes

In this chapter, you will find easy-to-follow recipes that you can make in your Electric Smoker. You must follow all recipes exactly according to the instructions for the best results.

102.   5.1. Beef BBQ Brisket

This is an easy recipe for BBQ brisket that you will prepare in your Electric Smoker. Be assured that you will enjoy the original BBQ flavor. The meat will have a beautiful texture on the outside and will be tender inside. Just follow the instructions carefully, and you are in for a treat. They this recipe and you will not be disappointed.

- Course: Dinner

- Cuisine: American BBQ

- Total Time: 8 hours 50 minutes

- Preparation Time: 30 minutes

- Cooking Time: 8 hours

- Rest Time: 20 minutes

- Serving Size: 2 servings

- Nutritional Value Per Serving

  - Calories: 564 calories

  - Carbohydrates: 0 g

  - Protein: 77.3 g

  - Fats: 27.4 g

Equipment Used:

- Electric Smoker

Ingredients:

1. BBQ rub (store-bought) 5 tbsp.
2. Beef Brisket ½ kg.

Instructions:

- Preheat the electric Smoker at 225°F.

- Then prepare the beef brisket. Wash the meat and pat it dry.

- Trim all the excess fat from the brisket, leaving only one-fourth of an inch of fat on the meat.

- Next, remove the excess skin from the underside of the meat cut.

- Now, apply the BBQ rub on the beef on both sides generously.

- Put the brisket in the Electric Smoker and insert the probe in the thickest part of the beef.

- Smoke the beef until the temperature has reached 160°F. This usually takes six hours. It might take longer, so you must see when the temperature reaches a certain point.

- At this stage, please take out the brisket very carefully and wrap it tightly in aluminum foil.

- Place it back into the Smoker and wait until the brisket's temperature reaches 190°F. This usually takes additional 2 hours. The time might be a bit more depending on the brisket.

- When the beef is at 190°F, take it out of the Smoker.

- Let it rest for 20 to 30 minutes.

- Then unwrap the brisket and slice it.

- Enjoy the delicious BBQ brisket.

5.2.   Smoked Salmon

The best thing about this recipe is that it is easy to make and quick to prepare. Minimum ingredients are used to achieve perfection with this smoked salmon. Try this recipe, and you will be in for a mouthwatering treat.

- Course: Lunch

- Cuisine: American

- Total Time: 2 hours 10 minutes

- Preparation Time: 10 minutes

- Cooking Time: 1 hour

- Rest: 20 minutes

- Serving Size: 3 servings

- Nutritional Value Per Serving

  - Calories: 454 calories

  - Carbohydrates: 0 g

  - Protein: 57.5 g

  - Fats: 24.2 g

Equipment Used:

- Electric Smoker

Ingredients:

1. Fresh Salmon 1 kg.

2. Brown Sugar 2 tbsp

3. Dried Dill 1 tsp

4. Pepper 1 tsp

5. Salt 1tsp

Instructions:

- Wash and pat dry the fish carefully. You must be careful with raw fish meat because it is delicate and can break.

- Mix the salt, pepper, sugar, and dill in a bowl.

- Rub this sugar mixture on the top side of the fish.

- Put it in the refrigerator for one hour. This will allow the fish to dry brine.

- Preheat the Electric Smoker at 250°F.

- Place a probe into the thickest part of the meat.

- Let it smoke until the meat reaches 145°F. It takes about 45 minutes to one hour.

- The dish can be served at room temperature or even cold.

- For this specific dish, you can use pecan, cherry, or oak wood for a subtle flavor.

5.3. Smoked Chicken

Chicken is one of the most widely popular food throughout the world. This recipe gives smoked chicken a spicy and flavorful twist. The brown sugar used in the rub gives it a caramelized look and texture and adds richness to the taste. Try this recipe out and you will not be disappointed.

- Course: Dinner

- Cuisine: American BBQ

- Total Time: 5 hours

- Preparation Time: 30 minutes

- Cooking Time: 4 hours

- Rest Time: 30 minutes

- Serving Size: 4 servings

- Nutritional Value Per Serving

  - Calories: 240 calories

  - Carbohydrates: 0 g

  - Protein: 21 g

  - Fats: 17 g

Equipment Used:

- Electric Smoker

Ingredients:

1. Medium sized whole chicken with skin

2. Thyme 1 tbsp

3. Cayenne Pepper 2 tbsp

4. Garlic Powder 1 tbsp

5. Chili Powder 2 tbsp

6. Salt 1 tbsp

7. Sugar 2 tbsp

8. Onion Powder 1 tbsp

9. Black Pepper 2 tbsp

10. Olive Oil 3 tbsp

Instructions:

- Arrange the woodchips in the electric smoker tray. You can use peach, apple, or cherry woodchips. Then turn on the electric Smoker to preheat at 225∘F.

- In a medium-sized mixing bowl, mix the thyme, cayenne pepper, garlic powder, chili powder, salt, sugar, onion powder, and black pepper. This will make the perfect rub for the chicken.

- First, rub the whole chicken with olive oil. All sides and inside the hollow cavity of chicken as well.

- After that, apply the prepared rub on the chicken generously. Rub it on the entire surface of the chicken.

- Put the skin over the breast of the chicken and apply the rub under the skin as well.

- Put the prepared chicken in the electric Smoker and insert a probe in the thigh.

- Check the chicken after every hour and take it out when the meat's internal temperature reaches 164∘F. The whole process takes about 4 hours.

- Served the smoked chicken warm.

5.4.   Smoked Corn on the Cob

Corn on the cob is a crowd's favorite side dish. It is popular among kids and adults alike. These complement all sorts of meats in a barbecue and give us that much-needed light and sweet flavors in the middle of a high protein barbecue. Try this easy recipe, and you will not regret preparing some smoked corn on the cob.

- Course: Side Dish

- Cuisine: American

- Total Time: 5 hours 10 minutes

- Preparation Time: 4 hours

- Cooking Time: 1 hour

- Rest Time: 10 minutes

- Serving Size: 6 servings

- Nutritional Value Per Serving

  - Calories: 142 calories

  - Carbohydrates: 16.6 g

  - Protein: 2.7 g

  - Fats: 8.6 g

Equipment Used:

- Electric Smoker

Ingredients:

1. Ear corn with husks 6 pieces

2. Brown sugar 2 tbsp

3. Salt ½ tsp

4. Garlic powder ½ tsp

5. Melted butter ¼ cup.

6. Onion powder 1 tsp

7. Sliced green onion 3 pieces.

Instructions:

- Take a large roasting pot and fill it half with room temperature water.

- Pull the husks of all the corn cobs and remove the silks. Let the husks remain attached to the cob but just pulled back.
- Soak the corn cobs in the water and if needed, fill the pot with more water to completely immerse the cobs into water.
- Soak for 4 hours.
- After that remove, the cobs from the pot and place them on paper towels and let them dry.
- Preheat the electric Smoker at 225°F. Place the woodchips inside the electric Smoker.
- In a mixing bowl, mix the butter, sugar, salt, onion powder, and garlic powder to make a rub for the corn on the cob.
- With the help of a brush, apply the rub generously to the corn cobs.
- Pull the husks back on the corn cobs. Place them in the electric Smoker.
- Leave for 60 minutes and then take them out.
- Let them rest for 10 minutes, and then serve them as a delicious side dish.

5.5. Grilled Chicken Thighs with Asparagus

This delicious chicken recipe is perfect for enjoying on the weekend. It is easy to make and takes only 2 hours to prepare. The juicy chicken with the light smokiness is a success with kids and adults alike. This dish will be a crowd favorite. Try out this recipe and enjoy it with friends and family.

- Course: Lunch

- Cuisine: American

- Total Time: 5 hours

- Preparation Time: 3 hours

- Cooking Time: 2 hours

- Rest Time: 10 minutes

- Serving Size: 3 servings

- Nutritional Value Per Serving

  - Calories: 482 calories

  - Carbohydrates: 58.8 g

  - Protein: 58.5 g

  - Fats: 19.3 g

Equipment Used:

- Electric Smoker

Ingredients:

For Chicken:

1. Chicken thighs 3 to 4 pieces
2. Store-bought BBQ rub 5 tbsp.
3. Water as required.
4. Sugar 1 tsp
5. Salt 1 tsp
6. ¼ cup apple cider vinegar

For Asparagus

1. Asparagus 1 bunch
2. Red pepper flakes 1 tsp
3. Balsamic Vinegar ¼ cup
4. Pepper 1 tsp
5. Salt 1 tsp

Equipment Used:

- Electric Smoker

Instructions:

- Prepare to brine the chicken thighs. Put the chicken in a large zip lock bag, then add Vinegar, salt, and sugar.
- Then, fill the bag with water such that the chicken pieces are completely soaked. Put it in the refrigerator for 2 to 3 hours.

- The brining process will ensure that the chicken does not dry out while in the electric Smoker.

- Similarly, prepare a marinade for the asparagus bunch as well. Please put it in a large zip lock bag. Add the balsamic vinegar, salt pepper, pepper flakes and water to soak the asparagus. Please leave it in the refrigerator for 3 hours.

- Prepare a small BBQ spray bottle having one part vinegar, two parts water and 1 tsp sugar. Mix it properly. This will be used to spray on the chicken while it is being smoked.

- Take the chicken out of the refrigerator after 2 hours and wash and dry the pieces.

- Apply the BBQ rub generously on the chicken pieces.

- Preheat the electric Smoker at 225°F for 15 minutes. Put the apple woodchips in the wood tray.

- Place the chicken thighs in the electric Smoker.

- Spray with the BBQ spray bottle after every 20 to 30 minutes. This will prevent the chicken from drying.

- Smoke the chicken for about two hours.

- Take the chicken out of the Smoker and let it rest for 10 minutes.

- Meanwhile, please take out the asparagus and spread it on a paper towel and pat dry.

- Put the asparagus in the electric Smoker and leave for 10 minutes, and then take it out.

- Serve the chicken with a side of asparagus.

- This is a good pairing to serve, and the asparagus complements the smoked chicken beautifully.

Turkey has often been bland and boring meat. This recipe gives the turkey a tasty and spicy twist. The BBQ sauce mixed with hot sauce and honey gives the smoked turkey a rich flavor and an amazing texture. Try out this mouthwatering and delicious recipe and enjoy the aromatic and tender turkey meat. This recipe never disappoints.

- Course: Lunch
- Cuisine: American
- Total Time: 3 hours 20 minutes
- Preparation Time: 5 minutes
- Cooking Time: 3 hours
- Resting Time: 10 minutes

- Serving Size: 3 to 4 servings
- Nutritional Value Per Serving
  - Calories: 380 calories
  - Carbohydrates: 16.5 g
  - Protein: 28.2 g
  - Fats: 20.8 g

Equipment Used:

- Electric Smoker

Ingredients:

1. Turkey breast 1 piece
2. Store-bought BBQ rub 4 tbsp.
3. Olive oil 3 tbsp.
4. Butter 100 g
5. Hot Tabasco sauce 2 tsp
6. Honey 1tsp

Instructions:

- First, preheat the electric Smoker at 250°F for at least 15 minutes.
- Put in the mesquite woodchips in the Smoker.
- Next, prepare the turkey meat. Cover the whole meat with a layer of olive oil. Rub the oil generously.
- Then apply the BBQ rub on the whole meat piece. Rub the mixture generously so that the whole turkey breast is covered with the BBQ rub.

- In a heatproof cup, prepare the basting mixture for the turkey. Add the butter, cut into small cubes to the cup. Put in the honey, hot sauce and ¼ teaspoon BBQ rub.

- Put the turkey and the cup in the electric Smoker and let it remain closed for approximately 45 minutes. Put a probe in the turkey meat at the thickest part of the meat.

- When you open the electric Smoker after 45 minutes, you will see that the basting mixture is prepared and is steaming.

- Pour the basting mixture about 2 tbsp on the meat and let it smoke.

- Repeat the procedure with the basting mixture after every 20 minutes.

- When the internal temperature of meat is near 170∘F, raise the electric Smoker's heat to 270∘F for the last 10 minutes.

- Take out the meat when the internal temperature reaches 170∘F.

- Let the meat rest for 15 minutes and then slice it.

- Serve this mouthwatering and delicious meal to your friends and family.

5.7. Smoked Potatoes

Baked potatoes are an all-time favorite side dish. They go well with all meats, especially chicken. They can be served as it is or with a rich sour cream. This is an easy and useful recipe to smoke potatoes perfectly. This recipe is simple and easy to prepare and goes well with almost anything. You can even make this and have it on its own. It is great comfort food. Try it out and you will not be disappointed.

- Course: Side Dish

- Cuisine: American

- Total Time: 2 hours 20 minutes

- Preparation Time: 10 minutes

- Cooking Time: 2 hours

- Rest Time: 10 minutes

- Serving Size: 4 servings

- Nutritional Value Per Serving

  - Calories: 119 calories

  - Carbohydrates: 10 g

  - Protein: 1.8 g

  - Fats: 8.5 g

Equipment Used:

- Electric Smoker

Ingredients:

1. Medium sized potatoes 4 pieces
2. Olive oil ¼ cup
3. Granular Salt ¾ cup

Instructions:

- Preheat the electric Smoker at 275°F. Put in the wood chips of your choice. Preheat for at least 15 minutes.
- Wash the potatoes and dry them on a paper towel.
- Poke each potato with a fork 5 or six times at different places on the potato surface. This will prevent the potato from exploding when it is exposed to a high temperature in the electric Smoker.
- Pour the oil in an open cup and coat each potato with a thin layer of oil.
- Next, pour the salt into a shallow dish. Coat the potatoes with this salt.
- Place the potatoes in the electric Smoker and wait for approximately 2 hours.
- After 2 hours, check the potatoes for doneness. The potatoes should be cooked and soft.
- Take the potatoes out and let them rest for 10 minutes.
- Slit the potatoes from the entrance and fill them with American-style chili if you want to serve as a main dish.
- Another serving idea is to slit the center and fill it with sour cream and top it with sliced green onions. This makes a perfect side dish.

5.8. Smoked Burgers

Burgers are a staple food in American cuisine. These smoked beef burgers have a smoky flavor and are perfect for a quiet weekend lunch with the family. The burgers do not have a sauce but are still delicious and mouthwatering. The best part about this recipe is that it is easy to make, and it takes less time for preparation and cooking. Try this recipe and enjoy it with friends and family.

- Course: Lunch
- Cuisine: American
- Total Time: 1 hour 20 minutes
- Preparation Time: 10 minutes
- Cooking Time: 1 hour

- Rest Time: 10 minutes

- Serving Size: 6 servings

- Nutritional Value Per Serving

  - Calories: 160 calories

  - Carbohydrates: 1 g

  - Protein: 11 g

  - Fats: 11 g

Equipment Used:

- Electric Smoker

Ingredients:

1. Pre-prepared beef burger patties 6 pieces

2. Salt 2 tbsp

3. Garlic Powder ½ tbsp

4. Pepper 1 tbsp

5. Dehydrated onion ½ tbsp

Instructions:

- Make sure that the burger patties are at room temperature.

- In a mixing bowl, add the salt, pepper, garlic powder, and dehydrated onion. Mix these ingredients well such that a rub is formed.

- Apply this rub on the burger patties. Cover both sides of the burger patty with the rub.

- Preheat the electric Smoker at 275°F for 15 minutes. Add the woodchips to the electric Smoker.

- Next, place the burger patties in the Electric Smoker.

- If you want your burger to be medium-well done, smoke for 45 minutes and if you want it to be well done, smoke for 60 minutes. This depends entirely on your preference.

- Once the patties are cooked, take them out of the Smoker and let them rest for 10 minutes.

- Next, prepare the buns and put them in the burger patties. These can be served as it is or some raw vegetables and sauce can be added.

5.9.   Smoked Chicken Drumsticks

This is a recipe for mouthwatering and flavorful drumsticks. The flavors are sweet and spicy. This recipe is prepared in 2 ½ hours, and you can enjoy these tasty drumsticks with BBQ sauce. Do try this recipe; this is a hit among kids and adults alike.

- Course: Dinner
- Cuisine: American
- Total Time: 3 hours

- Preparation Time: 15 minutes

- Cooking Time: 2 hours 30 minutes

- Serving Size: 6 persons

- Nutritional Value Per Serving

    - Calories: 180 calories

    - Carbohydrates: 8 g

    - Protein: 17 g

    - Fats: 8 g

Equipment Used:

- Electric Smoker

Ingredients:

1. Chicken Drumsticks 1.5 kg.
2. Store-bought Steak Rub ½ cup.
3. Cayenne Pepper 1 tsp
4. BBQ sauce ½ cup
5. Tabasco sauce 5 tbsp

Instructions:

- Wash and pat dry the drumsticks.

- Do not remove the skins from the chicken drumsticks.

- Rub the drumsticks with the store-bought steak rub and the cayenne pepper. Keep the drumsticks in the refrigerator for 2 hours.

- After a while, prepare the Electric Smoker.

- Put in the apple woodchips for a mild smoky flavor.

- Fill in the water tray with cold water.

- Turn on the electric Smoker at 250∘F to preheat.

- In the meanwhile, arrange the drumsticks in a stainless-steel wings rack.

- Put in the drumsticks in the Smoker and leave for 2 hours.

- At the end of 2 hours, check the internal temperature of drumsticks. The drumsticks are ready when the thermometer shows 160∘F as the internal temperature of the meat.

- Take out the drumsticks and let them rest for 5 minutes.

- Meanwhile, mix the BBQ sauce and tabasco sauce in a bowl.

- Dip all the drumsticks in the sauce one by one and arrange them on a platter.

- Serve hot.

5.10. Smoked Mac and Cheese

Mac and cheese as comfortable as comfort foods get. It serves as a great side dish with your barbeque. It is conventionally made in an oven, but you can also use a smoker to prepare this dish to give an extra smoky richness.

- Course: Side Dish

- Cuisine: American

- Total Time: 2 hours 30 minutes

- Preparation Time: 30 minutes

- Cooking Time: 2 hours

- Serving Size: 4 servings

- Nutritional Value Per Serving

  - Calories: 380 calories

  - Carbohydrates: 50 g

  - Protein: 8 g

  - Fats: 4 g

Equipment Used:

Electric Smoker

Ingredients:

1. Elbow Macaroni 1 packet, about ½ kg
2. Milk 3 cups
3. Flour ¼ cup
4. Cheese of your choice (grated) 500 g.
5. Cream cheese 250 g
6. Butter ¼ cup
7. Salt to taste
8. Pepper to taste

Instructions:

- First, boil 12 cups of water in a medium cooking pot. When the water comes to a boil, add the elbow macaroni, and let it boil for 8 to 10 minutes. When the macaroni is boiled, remove all the water, and put the macaroni aside.
- Next, you will prepare the cheese sauce.
- In a medium-sized pan, put in the butter in melt it over the flame. After the butter is melted, add the flour, and mix it. Cook for about two minutes till the flour starts to brown.
- Next, add the milk and cook for five minutes with constant stirring or whisking to not form lumps. Let the milk thicken. When the milk starts to thicken, take the saucepan off the flame, and add cream cheese.
- Mix the cream cheese and make a smooth mixture.
- In a heat-resistant bowl, add the cheese. Pour this mixture over the cheese and mix well.

- At this point, prepare the electric Smoker and put it to preheat at 225°F.

- Now take an aluminum tray and spread the cooked macaroni in its base.

- Pour the cream and cheese mixture over the macaroni such that it is fully immersed in the mixture.

- Put the aluminum tray in the Smoker for two hours.

- Take out the dish after two hours. The upper layer will come out crusty with cheesy and gooey richness beneath.

- Enjoy your mac and cheese separately or with barbequed chicken or meat.

5.11. BBQ Smoked Ribs

If you are someone who enjoys the ribs on the bone, this recipe is just for you. You will enjoy the rich smokiness of the ribs flavored with mild herbs served with BBQ sauce. Preparing BBQ ribs might be a bit tricky if you go the conventional way, but the ribs prepared in the electric Smoker save you all the hassle, giving you the same flavor.

- Course: Dinner

- Cuisine: American

- Total Time: 4 hours 30 minutes

- Preparation Time: 30 minutes

- Cooking Time: 4 hours

- Rest Time: 15 minutes

- Serving Size: 4 servings

- Nutritional Value Per Serving

    - Calories: 302 calories

    - Carbohydrates: 0 g

    - Protein: 22 g

- Fats: 23 g

Equipment Used:

- Electric Smoker

Ingredients:

1. One cut of ribs 1.5 kg
2. Black pepper 1 tsp
3. Paprika 1 tsp
4. Garlic Powder 2 tsp
5. Brown Sugar ¼ cup
6. Salt 1 tsp
7. BBQ sauce ¼ cup

Instructions:

- Prepare the ribs. Trim the extra fat and cut the ribs to easily fit on the Electric Smoker grills.
- Next, prepare the rub for the ribs. In a bowl, mix the pepper, paprika, salt, garlic powder, brown sugar, and salt.
- Rub this mixture on the ribs generously such that all parts of the ribs are rubbed with the herbs.
- Put the ribs in a large zip lock bag and put them in the refrigerator overnight.
- The next day, prepare the electric Smoker with applewood chips. Fill the water tray and turn on the Smoker at 225∘F.
- Let the Smoker preheat for 20 minutes.
- Bring out the ribs and arrange them in the smoker racks.

- Place them in the Smoker and let them smoke for 2 hours.

- After 2 hours, take them out, wrap them in aluminum foil, and put them back in the Electric Smoker.

- Let them smoke for a further two hours.

- Take the ribs out and let them rest for 15 minutes.

- After that, unwrap the ribs and serve.

5.12. Smoked Beef Jerky

Commercially prepared beef jerky is commonly available in the market. But there is nothing as flavorful and delicious as homemade beef jerky. In this recipe, we will learn how to prepare beef jerky from scratch.

- Course: Snack

- Cuisine: American

- Total Time: 5 hours

- Preparation Time: 30 minutes

- Cooking Time: 3 hours
- Resting Time: 1 hour
- Serving Size: 5 servings
- Nutritional Value Per Serving
  - Calories: 240 calories
  - Carbohydrates: 1 g
  - Protein: 50 g
  - Fats: 4 g

Equipment Used:

- Electric Smoker

Ingredients:

1. Round beef steak 1.5 kg
2. Honey ¼ cup
3. Soy sauce ¼ cup
4. Worcestershire sauce ¼ cup
5. Brown sugar ¼ cup
6. Garlic Powder 2 tsp
7. Red pepper flakes 1 tbsp
8. Salt 1 tsp
9. Onion Powder 2 tsp

Instructions:

- First, prepare the beef by trimming the extra fat and skin from the meat.
- Next, cut the meat into ¼ inch slices. Make sure that the slices are evenly cut.

- Set the meat aside.

- In a medium-size saucepan, add the honey, soy sauce, Worcestershire sauce, pepper, salt, garlic powder, onion powder, and sugar. Simmer it over the flame until a uniform mixture is formed.

- Let the mixture reach room temperature. Apply the mixture generously on the beef slices and put them in a zip lock bag.

- Pour the remaining sauce into the zip lock bag. Let it in the refrigerator overnight.

- The next day, prepare the electric Smoker with wood chips and water. Turn on the heat at 175∘ F and preheat for 10 minutes.

- Meanwhile, take out the beef slices and set them on a tray and let them reach room temperature.

- After that, arrange them in an aluminum tray and put them in the Smoker.

- Let the beef smoke for 3 hours.

- Take it out after three hours and rest for about 2 to 3 hours until it becomes dry.

- You can consume it as a snack and store it in an airtight container for up to 2 weeks.

5.13. Striped Bass Recipe

This is a delicious recipe having a mouthwatering flavor. Smoking the fish gives a much better flavor than just grilling. The smokiness makes this dish worth enjoying on a warm summer day. You can have it with a rich tartar sauce, or a little lime juice drizzled on it. If you try this recipe, you are in for a treat.

- Course: Lunch

- Cuisine: American

- Total Time: 3 hours

- Preparation Time: 45 minutes

- Cooking Time: 2 hours

- Serving Size: 6 servings

- Nutritional Value Per Serving

    - Calories: 154 calories

    - Carbohydrates: 0 g

    - Protein: 4 g

    - Fats: 28 g

Equipment Used:

- Electric Smoker

Ingredients:

1. Striped Bass Fillets 1 kg

2. Brown Sugar ¼ cup

3. Water 4 cups

4. Salt ¼ cup

5. Bay leaves 2 leaves.

6. Black pepper 2 tsp

7. Lemon 5 to 6 slices

8. Dry wine ½ cup for brine ½ cup for Smoker

9. Olive oil 3 tsp

Instructions:

- Clean and wash the fish fillets.

- Heat the four cups of water and dissolve salt and sugar in them. Let it come to room temperature.

- When it is at room temperature add, bay leaves, pepper, wine, and lemon slices.

- Put in the fish fillets inside this brine such that they are completely soaked.

- Cover them and leave them overnight.

- The next day prepares the Electric Smoker. Put the alder woodchips in the tray. Fill the water tray half with water and half with white wine.

- Turn on the burner at 180∘F.

- Bring out the fish fillets and take them out of the brine and wash them with cold water. Ste them on the counter on a tray lined with paper towels. Let them dry and come to room temperature.

- Meanwhile, coat the smoker grills with olive oil.

- When the fish fillets have reached room temperature, set them on the grills and smoke for two hours.

- The doneness is checked by inserting a thermometer; the internal temperature should be 145∘F.

- Please take out the fish and let it rest for 10 minutes before serving.

5.14. Smoked Cajun Shrimp

Shrimps are a crowd favorite seafood. They are easy to make, and preparation also takes a few minutes. Either you are using fresh shrimps or frozen ones, this recipe works best for both. The only thing is that for frozen shrimps, you will have to defrost them first. This recipe is easy and simple to follow and seldom goes wrong. You will thank us when you have tried this one.

- Course: Appetizer

- Cuisine: American

- Total Time: 1 hour

- Preparation Time: 20 minutes

- Cooking Time: 30 minutes

- Serving Size: 6 servings

- Nutritional Value Per Serving

  - Calories: 92 calories

- Carbohydrates: 2.2.g
- Protein: 4.6 g
- Fats: 7.6 g

Equipment Used:

- Electric Smoker

Ingredients:

1. Jumbo Shrimps 1 kg
2. Salt ¼ cup
3. Dried thyme 2 tbsp
4. Paprika 3 tbsp
5. Cayenne Pepper 2 tsp
6. Onion Powder 2 tbsp
7. Black Pepper 3 tbsp
8. Garlic Powder 2 tbsp
9. Olive Oil 3 tbsp
10. Lemon Juice ¼ cup
11. Fresh Parsley 1 bunch chopped.

Instructions:

- Prepare the shrimps. Take out the shells and devein them. Wash and pat them dry.
- In a bowl prepare the dry rum. Add salt, sugar, cayenne pepper, paprika, garlic powder, thyme, and onion powder. Mix this carefully.
- Next, prepare an aluminum tray by greasing it with olive oil.

- Place the shrimps on the tray in a single layer.

- Apply the dry rum to the shrimps generously.

- Start the electric Smoker at 225°F. Put in the wood chips and water.

- Let it preheat for 20 minutes.

- Meanwhile, pour lemon juice over the shrimps.

- Put the shrimps in the oven for thirty minutes, moving them after every ten minutes.

- Please take out the shrimps after 30 minutes or as soon as they start turning pink.

- This dish can be served warmed or even at room temperature.

5.15. Smoked Scallops

Scallops are juicy and delicious, either grilled or cooked. In this recipe, we have smoked the scallops to give them a rich smokiness. The scallops can be enjoyed with a side of a fresh green salad. This is the ultimate healthy dish to eat for lunch. Do try it out for a different and mouthwatering experience. You will not be disappointed.

- Course: Appetizer
- Cuisine: American
- Total Time: 50 minutes
- Preparation Time: 5 minutes
- Cooking Time: 30 to 40 minutes
- Serving Size: 5 servings
- Nutritional Value Per Serving
  - Calories: 105 calories
  - Carbohydrates: 5 g
  - Protein: 8.7 g
  - Fats: 5.3. g

Equipment used:

- Electric Smoker

Ingredients:

1. Sea Scallops 1 kg
2. Olive oil 3 tbsp
3. Salt 1 tsp
4. Garlic 2 cloves minced.
5. Pepper 1 tsp

Instructions:

- Wash the scallops under cold running water and dry them on a paper towel.
- In a bowl, mix the oil, salt, pepper, and lemon juice.
- Apply the mixture to the scallops.

- Turn on the electric Smoker and prepare it with water and add the wood chips.
- Let it preheat for 10 minutes at 225∘F.
- Meanwhile, lightly grease an aluminum pan and place the scallops on it such that the scallops do not touch each other.
- Put the scallops in the Smoker and smoke for 20 to 30 minutes.
- Check the internal temperature of the scallops.
- Take them out when the temperature reaches 145∘F.
- Let the scallops rest for 10 minutes and then serve with a fresh green salad and a vinaigrette.

104.   Smoked Curried Almonds

Almonds are an extremely healthy source of good fats. One enjoys munching them around. This recipe tries a twist on the good old roasted almonds. Let us make snack time fun with these delicious smoked curried almonds. You can keep them for as long as a month and keep enjoying a fistful every day. Heath and taste go hand in hand with this yummy snack.

- Course: Snack

- Cuisine: American

- Total Time: 1 hour 5 minutes

- Preparation Time:5 minutes

- Cooking Time: 1 to 2 hours

- Serving Size: 6 servings

- Nutritional Value Per Serving

    - Calories: 170 calories

    - Carbohydrates: 5 g

    - Protein: 6 g

    - Fats: 15 g

Equipment Used:

- Electric Smoker

Ingredients:

1. Raw Almonds with skins ½ kg
2. Butter 2 tbsp
3. Curry powder 2 tbsp
4. Raw Sugar 2 tbsp
5. 2 tbsp
6. Salt 1 tsp
7. Cayenne Pepper 1 tsp

Instructions:

- Preheat the electric Smoker at 225°F. Fill the water tray half with water and put in the pecan wood chips.
- In a large bowl, mix the butter, salt, sugar, cayenne pepper and curry powder.
- Toss all the almonds in this mixture.
- Prepare an aluminum tray, spread the almonds in the tray as a layer and put it in the Smoker.
- Leave the almonds for one hour and take them out.
- Delicious, curried almonds are ready.
- Let them rest to reach room temperature and enjoy this rich flavorful snack.
- These can be stored in an airtight container for up to 3 months.

If you have a sweet tooth and enjoy fruity desserts, this one is just for you. The naturally citrus flavor of apples is balanced perfectly with the sweetness of maple syrup and raisins. Do try out this recipe; you will not regret it.

- Course: Dessert

- Cuisine: American

- Total Time: 2 hours

- Preparation Time: 30 minutes

- Cooking Time: 1 hour 30 minutes

- Serving Size: 6 servings

- Nutritional Value Per Serving

  - Calories: 224 calories

  - Carbohydrates: 47 g

  - Protein: 1 g

  - Fats: 5 g

Equipment Used:

- Electric Smoker

Ingredients:

1. Apples 6 pieces
2. Maple Syrup ½ cup
3. Raisins ½ cup
4. Cold Butter ¼ cup cut in small cubes.

Instructions:

- Prepare the electric Smoker with water and pecan woodchips. Turn it on at 250°F.
- Take the apples, wash them, and pat dry. Core the apples such that their outer shape is maintained, and a small cavity is formed inside. The apple should still be able to stand without support.
- Fill the lower part of each apple with a small number of raisins, followed by some butter and then the maple syrup.
- Grease an aluminum tray and arrange the apples in the tray.
- Put the apples in the electric Smoker and let them smoke for 1 hour 30 minutes.
- Take them out and let them rest for 10 minutes.
- Serve warm with vanilla ice cream.

106.   Smoked Bean Sprouts

Bean sprouts are a great option for a side dish. They can be served with barbecued chicken and are a great source of vitamins and fiber. These are an excellent option for a side dish because they are easy to make and are prepared quickly.

- Course: Side Dish

- Cuisine: American

- Total Time: 1 hour 30 minutes

- Preparation Time: 15 minutes

- Cooking Time: 1 hour

- Serving Size: 6 servings

- Nutritional Value Per Serving

  - Calories: 45 calories

  - Carbohydrates: 8 g

  - Protein: 3 g

  - Fats: 0 g

Equipment Used:

- Electric Smoker

Ingredients:

1. Brussel Sprouts ½ kg
2. Olive Oil 3 tsp

3. Salt 1tsp

4. Pepper ½ tsp

Instructions:

- Wash the Brussel sprouts with cold water and dry them out in a colander.

- Remove the base of the Brussel sprouts and the dried-out parts.

- In a bowl, mix the olive oil, salt, and pepper.

- Apply the mixture to the sprouts and put them in a single layer in an aluminum tray.

- Turn on the electric Smoker at 225∘F. Prepare with water and wood chips.

- Let the Smoker preheat for 10 to 15 minutes and then put in the sprouts.

- Let them smoke for 60 minutes.

- Take them out and serve as a side dish with barbeque chicken.

107.   Smoked Cauliflower

Cauliflower is super healthy food. It is a rich source of vitamin C and dietary fiber. It contains eighty percent of the recommended amount of Vitamin C required for a day. It fills up your stomach and is slowly digested, thus keeping the stomach filled for a long while.

- Course: Side Dish

- Cuisine: American

- Total Time: 2 hours

- Preparation Time: 5 minutes

- Cooking Time: 2 hours

- Serving Size: 6 servings

- Nutritional Value Per Serving

    - Calories: 129 calories

    - Carbohydrates: 8 g

    - Protein: 3 g

    - Fats: 11 g

Equipment Used:

- Electric Smoker

Ingredients:

1. Cauliflower head 1 big
2. Salt 1 tsp
3. Olive Oil 3 tsp
4. Pepper 1 tsp
5. Balsamic Vinegar 3 tbsp

Instructions:

- Preheat the electric Smoker at 225°F. Fill the water tray and the woodchip tray accordingly.

- Cut the cauliflower head into small florets and wash them with cold water.

- In a bowl, mix the olive oil, balsamic vinegar, salt, and pepper.

- Toss the cauliflower florets in the bowl.

- In an aluminum tray, layer the cauliflower florets and put them in the Smoker.

- Smoke for 2 hours, turning the florets once midway.

- Take out after two hours and serve as a side dish.

5.20. Smoked Cherry Tomatoes

Smoked cherry tomatoes are not a dish in themselves but can form a base for other dishes like salads and pasta. This recipe is included here because smoked cherry tomatoes add flavor and richness to the foods they are mixed with. To add a rich smoky flavor to pasta, you can add cherry tomatoes. Adding smoked cherry tomatoes to a salad hive is the required kick to the otherwise boring salad. Smoked cherry tomatoes are uses as a side dish in Middle Eastern food commonly.

- Course: Side Dish

- Cuisine: American

- Total Time: 1 hour 5 minutes

- Preparation Time: 5 minutes

- Cooking Time: 1 hour

- Serving Size: 4 servings

- Nutritional Value Per Serving

  - Calories: 25 calories

  - Carbohydrates: 3.6 g

  - Protein: 1.1 g

  - Fats: 0.5 g

Equipment Used:

- Electric Smoker

Ingredients:

1. Cherry Tomatoes 300g

Instructions:

- Preheat the electric Smoker to 225∘F. Fill half of the water tray of the Smoker and fill in the wood chips.

- Wash the cherry tomatoes with cold water and spread them on a paper towel.

- Arrange the cherry tomatoes in the aluminum tray and put them in the Smoker.

- Leave the tomatoes for 60 minutes and then take them out.

- You will observe that the cherry tomatoes have burst open, and the juices are oozing out.

- Do not waste the juices; these juices also give off a smokey and delicious taste to salads and pasta.

5.21. Sweet and Spicy Chicken Wings

Chicken wings are another crowd favorite. This recipe used a lot of spices and cut the overpowering spicy flavor; sugar is used. The sugar gives a sweet taste and a crispy finish with its caramelization. This is a perfect dish if you are planning to host a barbecue party.

- Course: Lunch
- Cuisine: American
- Total Time: 1 hour 50 minutes
- Preparation Time:20 minutes
- Cooking Time: 1 hour 30 minutes
- Serving Size: 4 servings
- Nutritional Value Per Serving
  - Calories: 356 calories
  - Carbohydrates: 23.9 g
  - Protein: 15.6 g
  - Fats: 22.7 g

Equipment Used:

- Electric Smoker

Ingredients:

1. Chicken wings 2.5 kg
2. Salt 2 tsp
3. Pepper 1 tsp
4. Onion Powder 1 tsp
5. Garlic Powder 1tsp
6. Paprika ¼ cup
7. Cayenne Pepper 1 tsp
8. Brown Sugar ½ cup

Instructions:

- Wash the chicken wings with cold water and trim them.
- If you wish, you can break the wings in half or keep them full. Depends on your preference.
- Next, mix the paprika, salt, pepper, onion powder, garlic powder, sugar, and cayenne pepper in a big mixing bowl.
- Toss the chicken wings into this spice rub. Use your hands to coat the chicken wings with the spice rub.
- Turn on the electric Smoker at 250°F. Put water in the water tray and fill the wood chip tray with wood chips.
- Let the Smoker preheat for 15 minutes.
- Meanwhile, take out the grill from the Smoker and arrange the wings on the grill.

- Put in the wings in the Smoker and smoke for 2 hours. Check the internal temperature of the chicken should be 165°F.
- Take out the chicken wings and serve them hot.

5.22. Herbal Chicken Wings

This is a delicious recipe of chicken wings that has a strong flavor of herbs and spices. This recipe is inspired by French cuisine. Make this recipe to enjoy the Parisian feel in the comfort of your own house.

- Course: Lunch
- Cuisine: American
- Total Time: 3 hours 20 minutes

- Preparation Time: 10 minutes

- Cooking Time:

- Serving Size: 4 servings

- Nutritional Value Per Serving

    - Calories: 220 calories

    - Carbohydrates: 0 g

    - Protein: 18 g

    - Fats: 16 g

Equipment Used:

- Electric Smoker

Ingredients:

1. Chicken Wings 2.5 kg

2. Olive oil ½ cup

3. Garlic 2 cloves minced.

4. Rosemary Leaves 2 tbsp

5. Fresh basil leaves 2 tbsp.

6. Lemon Juice 2 tbsp

7. Salt 1 ½ tsp

8. Pepper 1tsp

9. Oregano 2 tbsp

Instructions:

- Prepare the chicken wings by trimming them. Wash the wings under cold running water.

- It is your choice to break the wings into half or use them as it is.

- In a large mixing bowl, add all ingredients and herbs and make a smooth mixture.

- Save half and toss the chicken wings in the other half.

- Use your hands to toss the wings in the mixture so that it is evenly applied.

- Preheat the electric Smoker at 250◦F and prepare it with water and wood chips.

- Arrange the wings on the smoker racks and smoke them for two hours.

- The doneness is determined by achieving a 165◦F temperature internally.

- Take out the wings and serve them hot.

5.23. Smoked Redfish

In this fish, we are using a dry brine technique. This is an easy and quick recipe; however, it requires the fish to marinate overnight. If you are planning to call guests over, you can prepare the fish fillets in advance.

- Course: Lunch

- Cuisine: American

- Total Time: 2 hours 10 minutes

- Preparation Time: 10 minutes

- Cooking Time: 2 hours

- Serving Size: 6 servings

- Nutritional Value Per Serving

    - Calories: 160 calories

    - Carbohydrates: 2 g

    - Protein: 18 g

    - Fats: 4 g

Equipment Used:

- Electric Smoker

Ingredients:

1. 2 redfish fillets with skin 600g
2. Salt half cup
3. Black pepper 1tsp
4. Lemon Zest 1 tsp
5. Garlic powder 1tsp
6. Lemon 2or 4 slices

Instructions:

- Wash the fish fillets with cold running water.

- Next, prepare a rub by mixing all the ingredients and spices.

- Apply the rub on the fish fillets generously. Wrap the fish fillets in cling film and refrigerate them overnight.

- The next day take out the fish fillets and bring them to room temperature.

- Prepare the electric Smoker with wood chips and water. Turn it on at 170◦F.

- When the fillets are at room temperature, wash them and pat them dry.

- Put them in the Smoker for two hours.

- After two hours, check the internal temperature. It should be 140◦F.

- Let the fillets rest for 30 minutes before serving.

5.24. Smoked Dory

This fish is easy to cook and quickly prepared. We will use the dry rub method to prepare the dory fish fillets. This turns out to be a delicious recipe and is a crowd favorite.

- Course: Dinner

- Cuisine: American

- Total Time: 1 hour 15 minutes

- Preparation Time: 15 minutes

- Cooking Time: 1 hour

- Serving Size: 4 servings

- Nutritional Value Per Serving

- Calories: 175 calories
- Carbohydrates: 2 g
- Protein: 22 g
- Fats: 8 g

Equipment Used:

- Electric Smoker

Ingredients:

1. 4 fillets of dory fish 800g
2. Onion Powder
3. Salt half cup
4. Black pepper 2tsp
5. Ginger powder 1 tsp
6. Garlic powder 1tsp
7. Coriander for garnish
8. Lemon slices for garnish

Instructions:

- Wash the fish fillets with cold running water.
- Next, prepare a rub by mixing all the ingredients and spices.
- Apply the rub on the fish fillets generously. Wrap the f·
  and refrigerate them overnight.
- The next day take out the fish fillets and bring '
- Prepare the electric Smoker with wood chips
- When the fillets are at room temperature, ·

- Could you put them in the Smoker for two hours?

- After one hour, check the internal temperature. It should be 160∘F.

- Let the fillets rest for 30 minutes before serving.

- Garnish the fish fillets with coriander and lemon slices for serving.

5.25. Herbal Smoked Salmon

Salmon is one fish variety that is consumed very often among people. The reason for this is that it is an excellent source of protein, and it cooks easily. Smoked salmon is something that you can enjoy at family dinners and other gatherings. You can never go wrong with smoked salmon.

- Course: Dinner

- Cuisine: American

- Total Time: 4 hours 30 minutes

- Preparation Time: 30 minutes

- Cooking Time: 4 hours

- Serving Size: 4 servings

- Nutritional Value Per Serving

- Calories: 210 calories

- Carbohydrates: 0 g

- Protein: 22.3. g
- Fats: 12.3 g

Equipment Used:

- Electric Smoker

Ingredients:

1. Salmon fillets 750 g
2. Salt ¼ cup
3. Sugar ¼ cup
4. Water ½ cup
5. Black Pepper 2 tbsp
6. Lemon 2 slices
7. Fresh dill chopped 1 bunch.

Instructions:

- Prepare the marinade for the fish. In a flat dish, pour water, salt, sugar, and pepper. Mix them well.
- Soak the fish fillets in the marinade and cover them with dill and lemon slices.
- Wrap the fillets in cling wrap and refrigerate overnight.
- The next day, prepare the Electric Smoker. Put the wood chips and water in the water tray.
- Turn on the electric Smoker at 180∘F. Put the fish fillets on the grill and smoke for four hours.

- In this recipe, we are smoking the fish at a lower temperature for a longer time. If you have a time constraint, you can use a higher temperature for a shorter period.

- Check the doneness of the fish by inserting the thermometer. The internal temperature must be 130◦F.

- Take out the fish and let it rest for 30 minutes before serving.

5.26. Smoked Stuffed Mushroom

These stuffed mushrooms can be served by themselves and can be served as a side dish as well. Try this recipe, and you will not be disappointed.

- Course: Side Dish

- Cuisine: American

- Total Time: 1 hour 15 minutes

- Preparation Time: 20 minutes

- Cooking Time: 55 minutes

- Serving Size: 6 servings

- Nutritional Value Per Serving

  - Calories: 320 calories

  - Carbohydrates: 22 g

- Protein: 8 g
- Fats: 7 g

Equipment Used:

- Electric Smoker

Ingredients:

1. Button Mushrooms with stem 24 mushroom
2. Onion 1 minced
3. Garlic 2 cloves minced.
4. Salt ½ tsp
5. Black Pepper 1 tsp
6. Breadcrumbs ¾ cup
7. Parmesan cheese ¾ cup
8. Olive Oil 1/3 cup
9. Parsley ¼ cup

Instructions:

- Preheat the electric Smoker at 250∘F. Put the wood chips in the tray and water in the water tray.
- In a saucepan, put in some olive oil and sauté the onion and garlic in it.
- In another mixing bowl, mix the breadcrumbs, cheese and salt and black pepper.
- Cut the stems of the mushrooms and chop them. Add the chopped stems to the saucepan with the onion and garlic and cook for one minute.
- Set an aluminum tray and set the mushroom heads up-side-down in a layer.

- Mix the onion, garlic, and mushrooms into the cheese mixture.

- Put a spoonful of mixture on the mushroom heads.

- Put the mushrooms in the Smoker and smoke for 45 minutes.

- Take out the mushrooms and let them rest for 20 minutes before serving.

5.27. Smoked Chicken Breast

This is a simple recipe and can never go wrong. Easy to make and delicious to taste. You can prepare this overnight and smoke it the next day. Family and friends will enjoy it alike.

- Course: Dinner

- Cuisine: American

- Total Time: 5 hours

- Preparation Time: 20 minutes

- Cooking Time: 4 hours 30 minutes
- Serving Size: 4 servings
- Nutritional Value Per Serving
  - Calories: 280 calories
  - Carbohydrates: 2 g
  - Protein: 23 g
  - Fats: 4 g

Equipment Used:

- Electric Smoker

Ingredients:

1. 4 chicken breast pieces 1 kg
2. Black pepper 2 tsp
3. Salt 2 tsp
4. Lemon Juice 4 tbsp
5. Paprika 2 tbsp

Instructions:

- Wash the chicken breast pieces. It is your choice to remove the skin or keep it.
- Pat the chicken dry.
- In a flat dish, mix the salt, pepper, paprika and lemon juice.
- Apply the mixture generously on the chicken and wrap the pieces with cling wrap and leave it in the refrigerator overnight.

- The next day, prepare the electric Smoker with the wood chips and water. Preheat the Smoker at 180◦F.
- Bring the chicken fillets at room temperature and wash them under cold running water.
- Pat the chicken dries with paper towels and arrange them on the racks of the Smoker.
- Smoke the chicken for about 4 hours and 30 minutes.
- Check the temperature of the chicken. It will be done when the internal temperature reaches 165◦F.
- Take out the chicken and let it rest for 30 minutes before serving.
- Serve with your choice of side dishes.

Introduction

Nutrition is crucial for athletes at the most fundamental level because it offers an energy source to conduct the task. Our power, preparation, productivity, and training are influenced by the meal we intake. Not only is the kind of food important to sports nutrition, but the times we consume across the day also affect our levels of performance and the ability of our bodies to recover after exercise. It's important to set your goals before you start eating the carnivorous diet method.

Keep in mind this is a change in lifestyle - no carbs, no plants, only products from animals and lots of good fat. You need to know why you are getting into the carnivore diet throughout the first place, whether it's to achieve your intended body weight, fight food allergies, decrease body fat battle with an autoimmune condition, and construct some muscular strength.

The Carnivore Diet arises from the widespread concept that mainly meat and fish were consumed by human ancestor communities and that high-carb diets are responsible for today's high rates of infectious disease.

Meals ingested before and after the workout are the most important thing about sports performance, but you should always be vigilant with all you put into your body. Athletes should eat around two hours before practicing as a general rule, and this diet should be low in fat, high in carbohydrates and high in protein.

The primary source of nutrition that drives your exercise schedule is protein, and carbohydrates are needed to help muscle recovery. You, therefore, need to replace the nutrients you have lost after exercising, and by incorporating protein in your post-workout meal, you need to allow consistent muscle recovery.

Chapter 1: What is the carnivore diet?

The Carnivore diet consists of foods dependent on animals, including fish, meat, low lactose milk and eggs products. Honey, zero carb seasoning, salt and pepper may also be used by a consumer pursuing the diet.

Certain items are eliminated from the diet, like grains, vegetables and fruits, plant-based oils, high lactose milk and carbohydrates.

The carnivore diet is based on the controversial theory that it was rich in meat eaten by human ancestors long ago. It assumes that when boosted by high protein and fat levels, human bodies operate best.

Figures such as Jordan Peterson (bestselling author and psychologist), Joe Rogan (standup comedian and podcast host), Shawn Baker (retired orthopedic surgeon) have made the diet popular.

On Carnivore Diet, once the appetite is satisfied, you eat fatty cuts of the high-quality meal and avoid all carbs, Sauces, Fruits, Nuts, Plant-based food, and Veggies.

Therefore, a carnivore diet is considered an "elimination diet" that can clarify its effectiveness in supporting others with digestive issues, constipation, and food sensitivities.

108.   1.1 How to organize your meal plan for your Carnivore Diet.

In Carnivore Diet, these tips have enabled us a great deal to remain encouraged and accomplish some auxiliary goals. That's the opportunity to get rid of extra fat, lose weight and attain that little muscular strength without missing the micronutrients needed. So, get into it now.

1. Know Your Why

It's necessary to set your objectives before you start your carnivore diet plan. Note that it is indeed a shift of lifestyle no carbs, no plants, just products from animals and lots of healthy fat. You have to remember why you are going into a carnivore diet from the first place, whether it's to achieve your target body weight, decrease body fat, battle digestive problems, cure an autoimmune condition, or create some lean muscle.

Depending on your needs, you have to assign yourself a clear goal. Perhaps it's about losing 20 lbs. Whether you go out on a summer break and acquire 5 pounds of muscle mass in six months - whatever it is, in the entire process, Stay close to the meat-only diet style.

It would be like a suggestion to help you stay on track to proceed with the carnivore diet. Whatever that is, to inform you of your diet pattern, experienced carnivore dieters may write it all down and upload it somewhere that you can see each day.

Based on your losing weight and other fitness objectives, it'll be like a way to remind you to keep you active to proceed with the carnivore diet.

2. Plan for sticking to The Meal Plan

It requires absolute devotion and determination to consume a moderate animal fat, carnivore diet for further than a few days or weeks. On the carnivore diet, the worst thing you can do is start taking it day by day and postpone it until the morning to find out what you're going to eat next. Instead, set specific targets for the week, use a diet planner, and list carnivore diet foods to schedule what animal products to consume in advance.

We also involve items like how many runs and visits to the workout we do, as well as what we'll have with each meal for our regular carnivore diet, in addition to having a carnivore diet food chart.

You may take some further time to discover new kinds of varieties of meat products you may like and methods of preparation to introduce a little more variety to your menu of animal meat. To try more diet choices and taste new tastes, you can also try on eating fresh animal organs (such as heart or cow liver). You can benefit from meal delivery if you are not dependent on cooking your foods while on the diet weight loss diet. It's an efficient method to reignite your Carnivore diet, and most significantly, according to your body's needs, you receive quality meats, pork, or chicken meat.

3.Preparations toward social life

The reality is that, on a carnivore diet, eating at social events seems to be one of the most disturbing situations. If you eat at a dinner party like that and tell people how every day eats lunch at McDonald's, eat Donuts and dinner pizza, you're not going to be judged more by people.

Suppose you tell another person on the table that you are on a carnivore diet meal schedule, though, because it includes eating only animal fat, zero plant foods and red meat because of your favorite diet. In that case, the entire table is now shocking. There's a vegetarian at the table, and Heaven forbid, you won't hear another word of it. Firstly, tell people you are doing so because of multiple problems with food allergies, and determining the underlying reasons, you are sticking with a carnivore diet.

Generally, at the start, we don't like speaking regarding weight loss. You'll only get remarks from several people so with this way, such as: "You're totally crazy not to eat fruit and veg, and it's so stupid." The vegetarian at the table will also have a lot of fruitier nutritional vocabulary and a long discussion about the need to eat fruit and veggies to get more nutrition. In this scenario, we find that asking if they are associated with their fitness or yours is the only solution that helps? It fits us nine times in a row, and if you get yourself sitting beside the vegetarian, then change the topic to another one.

4. Dining Out

The pleasant deal for people upon this carnivore diet is with quality nutrition meats that will suit your needs; there are many places you can eat out. Eating at BBQ and steak restaurants is probably the best decision you can make. But make sure to avoid animal meats that are frozen. In the carnivorous weight loss diet, consuming meat products is not tolerated. Everything you need to do is pay attention to the way the meals are prepared. While on a carnivore diet, the main thing is to avoid consuming something that includes stir-fried vegetables or sauces.

Unfortunately, in many Indian and Chinese restaurants, you'll most likely stop eating out for a carnivore diet because almost all their meals are heavy with sauces and salt. What we usually do when we start our all-meat diet is review the menus online. We'd be likely to eat there as long as we see filet mignon and are steaks accessible.

1.2 15 days meal plan for the Carnivore Diet.

Carnivore Diet For 1st week

On Monday

Breakfast 1 or 2 100 percent pure pork sausages (3 ounces) and Five bacon slices (about 4 ounces)

Lunch just 10 ounces of grilled beef patty burger with a slice of cheese.

Dinner four stacks of healthy lamb (12 ounces)

On Tuesday

Breakfast 3 bacon slices (4 ounces) 3 grilled 100 percent pure pork sausages (about 5 ounces)

Lunch Slammed buttery cutlets of salmon upon the bone (about 15 ounces).

Dinner Porterhouse steak (12 ounces) grilled with butter.

On Wednesday

Breakfast Grilled trout fillets with butter (about 10 ounces)

Lunch Grilled belly of pork (about 10 ounces)

Dinner Slow beef roast upper side (about 12 ounces)

On Thursday

Breakfast Roasted ground beef burger patty with cheese (about 8 ounces)

Lunch Roast salmon cutlets with butter on the bone (about 15 ounces)

Dinner Grilled steak porterhouse (about 12 ounces)

On Friday

Breakfast 2 breasts of grilled chicken with skin (about 8 ounces)

Lunch fillets of fried trout (about 16 ounces)

Dinner Slow grilled upper side of beef (about 12 ounces)

On Saturday

Breakfast three 100 percent pure pork sausages grilled (about 5 ounces)

Lunch Three slices of bacon (about 4 ounces) Four healthy lamb chops (about 12 ounces)

Dinner Grilled steak ribeye (about 12 ounces)

On Sunday

Breakfast two breasts of grilled chicken with skin (about 8 ounces)

Lunch 4 grilled or fried pork chops (about 12 ounces)

Dinner Grilled steak ribeye (about 12 ounces)

Shopping list for 1st week

- Pork belly about 10 ounces

- Lamb Chops about 24 ounces

- Beef Grounded about eighteen ounces

- Porterhouse steak about twenty-four ounces

- Topside of beef about twenty-four ounces

- Salmon cutlets about thirty ounces (or other fatty fish)

- Trout about twenty-six ounces

- Butter around one lb.

- Cheese around half lbs.

- Bacon about twelve ounces

- 100 percent pork sausages around 13 ounces

- Pork chops about twelve ounces

- Chicken breasts

- Ribeye steak about twenty-four ounces

- The top side of beef about twenty-four ounces

- salmon cutlets about thirty ounces (or any other fish with fats)

Carnivore diet meal plan for 2nd week

We will be reducing much of the milk from items on our carnivore diet during the next week. We're still going to allow the butter to be utilized for the food, but dairy foods such as cheese will now be gone.

On Monday

Breakfast Two breasts of grilled chicken with skin (about 8 ounces)

Lunch Slow beef grilled topside (about 12 ounces)

Dinner four healthy lamb pieces (about 12 ounces)

Tuesday

Breakfast roasted ground beef patty burger (about 8 ounces)

Lunch on the bone roasted salmon cutlets (about 15 ounces)

Dinner Grilled steak ribeye (about 8 ounces) and roasted liver of beef (about 4 ounces)

On Wednesday

Breakfast 5 bacon slices (about 4 ounces) and one- or two-100 percent pork sausages (about 3 ounces)

Lunch grilled porterhouse steak with butter (about 12 ounces)

Dinner Slow beef roast topside (about 12 ounces)

On Thursday

Breakfast Grilled steak with ribeye (about 12 ounces)

Lunch 3 chicken breasts grilled with skin (around 12 ounces)

Dinner barbequed ground beef patty burger (around 12 ounces)

On Friday

Breakfast sirloin steak grilled with butter (about 8 ounces)

Lunch Slow beef roast topside (about 8 ounces) and roasted liver of beef (4 ounces)

Dinner with four fried or grilled pork pieces (about 12 ounces)

On Saturday

Breakfast Grilled ground beef patty burger (about 8 ounces)

Lunch Roast salmon cutlets on the bone with butter (about 15 ounces)

Dinner Grilled steak of sirloin (12 ounces)

On **Sunday**

Breakfast Grilled steak ribeye (about 8 ounces)

Lunch Slow roast beef upside (about 12 ounces)

Dinner 3 grilled with skin chicken breast (about 12 ounces) and roasted liver of beef (about 4 ounces)

Shopping list for 2nd week:

- Salmon cutlets about thirty ounces or any other fatty fish

- Ribeye steak about twenty-eight ounces

- Pork chops around twelve ounces

- Beef's liver around twelve ounces

- Ribeye steak around twenty-four ounces

- 100 percent pork sausages about three ounces

- Porterhouse steak about twelve ounces

- Chicken breasts about thirty-two ounces

- Topside of beef around forty-four ounces

- Lamb chops around twelve ounces

109.   1.3 What food is included in the carnivore diet?

The Carnivore Diet falls completely under one category of food: animal products.

Though animal products can break into additional categories, there are various content standards within each category. Now let's look into those classifications.

MEAT

Any type: lamb, beef, poultry, pork etc. Preferably choose grass-fed or organic meats.

ORGANS

Organs are an excellent substitute but are a key element of a well-formulated carnivore diet. Try to include chicken liver, kidneys, beef heart, beef liver, and brains.

EGGS.

Eggs of all kinds from most birds. Where possible, choose organic.

FISH AND SEAFOOD

Choose fatty fish such as sardines, mackerel, salmon herring are great and might even have health privilege due to high amounts of omega-3 fatty acids. Other seafood includes shrimp, squid tilapia, tuna, swordfish, and trout scallops.

DAIRY

Choose full-fat options where possible, like full-fat cream, real butter, sour cream, high-fat cheeses, and Greek yogurt. Try to use skim milk minimum, reduced fat, and regular milk as they contain many sugars.

FATS AND OILS

For cooking, use ghee, butter, tallow, lard, chicken fat, suet and tallow duck fat.

CARNIVORE DRINKS

WATER

Wherever appropriate, water must be your first preference. Try sparkling water if you think you're going to struggle with your water intake.

BONE BROTH

Broth from any animal's bones will make a drink that is warm and comforting.

TEA

Tea would Be OK with a drop of cream or milk. Green tea is best with no milk.

COFFEE

Coffee with milk, Black coffee or coffee with cream is all fine. Remember that the cream provides extra calories that you do not account for when attempting to lose weight.

110.   1.4 What Food items avoided on the Carnivore diet?

The Carnivore Diet prohibits all food that does not come from animals.

Restricted foods include:

Vegetables: green beans, cauliflower, potatoes, broccoli, peppers, etc.

Legumes: lentils, beans, etc.

Nuts and seeds: sunflower seeds, pumpkin seeds, almonds, pistachios, etc.

Grains: quinoa, bread, pasta, rice, wheat, etc.

Alcohol: wine, liquor, beer, etc.

Sugars: maple syrup, brown sugar, table sugar etc.

"Beverages" other than water: coffee, tea, fruit juice, soda etc.

PROCESSED MEATS

Process meats are highly insufficient in diet and moderate in chemical substances.

LOW-FAT MILK.

High sugar usually consists of skimmed milk and low fat. Unless you need to, restrict it to a few drops in your coffee or tea.

Sauces & Seasoning

While seasoning a steak with thyme, salt, or even paprika is not unusual, going too deep on sauces and seasoning can cause stomach issues for those with a weak immune system.

Foods on the Carnivore Diet that might be OK.

Foods that may be permissible include:

Milk

Yogurt

Cheese

111.   1.5 How carnivore diets have beneficial effects?

The carnivore diet has helped thousands of people fix the effects of many health conditions or improve them. Check out some favorable circumstances of the carnivore diet.

Minimize Acid Reflux

As stomach acid rises into the esophagus, acid reflux occurs, causing discomfort that can lead to heartburn symptoms. In the United States, this is relatively a common medical complaint, and many of us live on the belief that there is little we can do to change it. Fortunately, that isn't valid.

Although no food form has yet been shown to cure this disorder entirely, your dietary choices will help minimize or even eradicate symptoms a great deal. That makes a decent amount of sense, provided that in your stomach, this condition begins.

IMPROVED ACNE

Acne, defined by the occurrence of spots mostly on the face, neck and shoulders and is also a sign of hormonal changes that causes inflammation elsewhere in the body. It can be physically and psychologically uncomfortable, depending on your diet, and it's avoidable.

There are several reasons why the carnivore diet helps hold spots at bay. The key theory connects carbohydrate intake and acne. Image Inflammation is a significant cause of acne as well. Incidentally, in those that eat so many carbohydrates, inflammation is identified.

Meat also provides vital nutrients, which have also been observed to affect breakouts, including omega 3s and zinc. Several meat substitutes, such as milk, can also worsen no-ending acne. If you want flawless skin, a carnivore diet could provide an alternative.

Maintain ADD/ADHD

Hyperactivity disorders that affect kids, teenagers, and even adults are called ADD and ADHD. Either syndrome may contribute to hyperactivity, impaired control of impulses, and trouble paying attention.

It is no secret that in problems such as these, diet plays a major role. Although many studies of ADHD and diet effects are still needed, the wrong foods appear to worsen troublesome symptoms.

The advantages of the carnivore diet have been shown to improve the symptoms. Perhaps because of the interaction of plant foods with the gut microbiome.

PREVENT ALZHEIMER'S

Alzheimer's is a steady brain disease that kills memory, cognitive capacity, and comprehension of even basic activities such as brushing teeth. It has a devastating effect on the lives of patients affected and on their loved ones and sometimes results in hospitalization or treatment for the long term.

The good news is that there is evidence to indicate a diet that can help with such a carnivore diet free of plant foods. Although there is no way to reverse the effect of Alzheimer's, modifying diets like this might minimize symptoms. Studies show that consuming a lower diet of plant foods over your life can also minimize the risk of Alzheimer's by up to 44%!

The association between the lectins present in plants and Alzheimer's is the key explanation why plant foods are causing concern. As such, patients who eat large quantities of plant food can intensify their symptoms and put themselves at risk. By contrast, healthy fats such as those present in beef can hold symptoms at bay and, as a result, delay Alzheimer's expansion.

IMPROVE BLOOD PRESSURE

Blood pressure associate with the pressure of circulating blood on the walls of blood vessels. Lifestyle and diet control of blood pressure is essential for ongoing health and the prevention of progressive health problems such as heart disease. While meat gave a bad perspective when it comes to blood pressure, it is not reasonable.

In terms of blood pressure regulation, limiting carbohydrate intake and consuming red meat and fish, turkey, or skinless chicken have shown positive results.

It is mainly due to high levels of protein present in animal foods, according to studies. There is also some evidence that a balanced intake of vitamin D and omega-3 will help maintain an even keel for blood pressure rates. Obviously, with a very well carnivore diet, they are simple enough to come by.

REDUCE CANCER RISK

A disease that no one wishes to obtain is cancer, marked by the uncontrolled division of cancerous cells. It's one of the most serious diseases we struggle with without a cure today, despite medical advances and increased recovery rates.

Our chances of developing cancer will affect our lifestyle. Smoking, for instance, increases the probability of irregular cells. What fewer people know is that cancer and what we eat also have close ties. Although research is underway on exactly what effect food can have, a balanced diet is important to keep this problem at bay.

In particular, studies have shown that diets that are low in carbohydrates and rich in healthy proteins may help keep the body fit and resistant to cancer growth. Red meat and poultry can provide any diet with a great deal of protein while also maintaining gut bacteria as safe for cancer-fighting potential as possible.

DIABETES CONTROL

Diabetes is a chronic disorder that impacts the body's ability to maintain the consumption of sugar.

Type 1 diabetes happens when the body's immune system kills cells that contain insulin.

Type 2 diabetes happens when a person does not, in the first place, generate enough insulin. This disease, as you are probably aware, occurs mainly in people with low, high-sugar diets. In reality, by simply changing what they eat, some individuals with type 2 diabetes might completely turn around. Management of diabetes is a considerable health improvement of carnivore diet, and it is not unbelievable to see that high-quality meat may help minimize sugar intake. That's because the protein found in red meats will hold the level of satiety stable for longer, often without causing blood pressure to increase. Zero carbs, which has been proven to be one of the effective methods of controlling blood glucose levels, is also a carnivore diet.

WEIGHT LOSS

While we're on the topic of losing weight, the carnivore diet has become just another possible health gain. In the U.S. alone, estimates that there are approximately 160 million people above.

It is a set of problems because overweight itself can contribute to many of the issues we have addressed here, including heart diseases, thyroid issues, and diabetes. Fortunately, meat has one of the planet's most weight-loss-friendly ingredients. That's why the carnivore diet is so satisfying for so many.

Thanks to its high nutritional value, lean beef has specifically been found to be useful here. A high-quality steak will keep you energized, manage blood sugar, and also ensure that you don't need to have a snack. Protein was quite good for this; in particular, research has shown that a 25 percent increase in protein can reduce cravings by 60 percent. Even better, to appreciate those all-important advantages, you don't need to compromise on taste.

CONSTIPATION RELIEF

Constipation refers to irregular bodily functions that are hard to get through. What we eat will play a major role in producing symptoms in a condition of this type. And you can guarantee that when you spend all night in the bathroom, you will regret those unhealthy choices.

In contrast, it will help to keep our digestive system normal and flowing by shifting our preference to constipation-friendly menus. That, in turn, if we put the effort in, will hold the C-word at bay for our entire lives for a long period.

Here, the carnivore diet is also helpful as it offers delicious, low fiber meals that ensure that things move for you. No studies support the argument that high in fiber foods are beneficial for digestive health, and zero fiber diets have shown the best improvements in some research.

EPILEPSY MANAGEMENT

Epilepsy disrupts the mechanisms of brain messaging and thus causes frequent seizures. Some patients will only have seizures in their childhood and teenage years, whereas others will continue to fight epilepsy through their lifetime. Epilepsy causes fluctuate and may include head injuries and disorders of the brain. However, you might be surprised to learn that specialists have found proven advantages for patients concentrating on dietary changes, particularly low-carb diets such as the carnivore diet. Eating just meat may have such an effect that certain patients can decrease or eliminate drugs and encounter fewer or no seizures. In situations like this, high-fat products such as hamburgers and bacon also seem to have the best outcomes. Although it is not generally understood why all these foods have such a major effect on seizures (up to a reduction of 90%!), the research suggests that it can make a huge difference to eat more fat and to steer clear of carbohydrates.

Reduce THYROIDs Problems

Thyroid issues come in a variety of forms and often occur due to thyroid hormone production issues. The overproduction of certain hormones is hyperthyroidism. When the thyroid stops producing enough hormones, hypothyroidism occurs. Problems such as these can be dangerous for patients, although they are fully treatable with hormone substitutes or, in several cases, diet.

Evidence indicates that it can go a long way to minimize or even avoid thyroid disorders by consuming a diet rich in unique nutrients. When you look at just what those nutrients are, it's obvious to see that most of them are in meat.

In particular, zinc can stimulate thyroid hormones in hypothyroidism and is not in short supply from a diet rich in beef. All meats are, in truth, recommended for those who need to increase the development of thyroid hormone. It's also worth noting that it has been shown that weight loss on a low-carb diet helps reduce the development of excess thyroid hormones. That implies that increased intake of meat will enhance this situation all around.

1.6 Side Effects of carnivore diet and their Cures?

Without its health consequences, no diet appears that's also part of the carnivore diet. Fortunately, on an animal-based diet, the human body performs exceptionally well, and any harmful side effects are temporary. Here are a few side effects of a carnivorous diet and how to treat them.

DIARRHEA ON CARNIVORE DIET

Your gastrointestinal tract may experience disruptions if you have diarrhea, feel uneasy in the bathroom, or get alarming signals from the digestive system.

What happens?

Diarrhea may happen when food moves too rapidly through your digestive tract. Transit times are typically slower if you've been consuming plant foods to give your body time to cope with the extra fiber and extract nutrients from the food. Transit time can be affected as you move to a zero-fiber diet and diarrhea occurs.

What's the effective cure?

On the carnivore diet, the treatment for diarrhea is:

Give your body time to adjust to a zero-fiber diet - food can move too quickly through the large intestine at first so that the large intestine pulls water from the food.

Minimize the intake of rendered fats - liquid fats such as tallow and cream are commonly rendered fats. These fat types can move too easily through your system.

BAD BREATH ON THE CARNIVORE DIET

One of the side effects of going from a high protein diet using glucose as the primary fuel source to a low carb diet while using ketones as a fuel source is bad breath. "The "keto breath" is often considered to.

What Happens?

Compound acetone is responsible for the change in the scent of your breath. Acetone is the simplest and perhaps most rapidly changing of the various forms of ketones and is formed from acetoacetate, ketone muscle dissolution. Acetone disperses into the lungs during ketosis and leaves the body as you exhale.

What's the effective cure?

Some individuals don't get a keto breath, but with time, it goes away on its own for those who do. If you do have it, during the carnivore diet, there are some things you can do to minimize bad breath.

Wait - if it's not that bad, sitting it out and waiting for it to go on its own is OK.

Drink more - As you urinate, ketones can often leave the body, so drinking more water will also eliminate extra ketones in the urine.

Stay fresh- Keep your teeth, tongue, gums, and mouth clean so the air you breathe does not mix with any other unpleasant odors.

HEART PALPITATIONS ON THE CARNIVORE DIET

The carnivore diet's common symptom is heart palpitations, beating heart, and flutters, but it is generally episodic and nothing to stress about in these situations.

What Happens

It's normal to find that your heart rate increases, or your stroke volume increases when you first adopt a carnivore diet. It is generally due to a lower blood volume, dehydration, and a loss of electrolytes, which can be the product of low blood volume. The heart needs to toughen up to work harder to maintain the blood pressure when you feel those fast heartbeats.

What's the effective cure?

Drinking enough water is the easiest cure and ensuring that you keep the salt your body requires will help fight those palpitations in the heart. Additional options include:

Take some magnesium - the recommended daily amount is up to 400 mg per day and is safe for most individuals.

Get on point with your salt intake - too little or too much can cause palpitations in the chest. It's probably more likely that you have too little rather than too many.

Add in carbs - You will need to add more carbs to raise blood flow if the heart palpitations do not go away within a few weeks.

HIGH CHOLESTEROL ON THE CARNIVORE DIET

What Happens?

The Carnivore Diet is high in sodium, cholesterol and fat, and the elevation of your cholesterol levels may be one of the diet's most important concerns. The rise in saturated fat increases your levels of cholesterol with time. Cholesterol, however, is not bad. The media and recent studies show that low carb and higher fat diets can contribute to an improved lipid profile.

What's the effective cure?

Before you start the carnivore diet, have your cholesterol levels tested first and foremost, so you have a baseline on which to operate. There are a few things you can do if you get a relevant lipid profile on the carnivore diet:

Reduce the consumption of liquid fat. It can also, on its own, boost your lipid profile.

For at least 12 hours a day, try fasting. There is sufficient evidence to suggest that this would lower total cholesterol levels.

Consult the physician. Most doctors are willing to speak with you about your carnivore way of life and give suggestions, particularly younger ones.

LEG CRAMPS ON CARNIVORE DIET

Among those who just started the carnivore diet, leg cramps are a frequent issue, but they typically fade over time. With that said, on the carnivore diet, there are some items you can do to avoid or remove leg cramps completely.

What Happens?

Muscle cramps are caused by the change of nutrients, especially magnesium. Consequently, it is also not unusual to get leg cramps due to low potassium or sodium intake.

What's the effective cure?

On the carnivore diet, leg cramps treatment is to even magnesium, sodium, and potassium levels. It can attain in two ways:

Increase sodium - Maybe the best way to balance your mineral levels is to add additional salt to your diet to avoid mineral loss. As levels of sodium decline, amounts of magnesium and potassium normally follow.

Supplement - consider replacing with magnesium in some situations where more sodium does not help.

Slow down - you might want some more time to adapt and in the worst situation where nothing works. Although pushing through is possible, it's also OK to add more carbs and then slowly decrease them over time to allow your body time to adjust.

Adaption: Nausea, Headaches, Lack of focus, Irritability

Due to your body's normal reaction to carbohydrate limitation and the elimination of unnecessary chemicals and additives, you will notice some unpleasant side effects and side symptoms during adaptation.

Some of the other effects of the adaption process include headache, chills, digestive issues, dizziness, irritability, bad breath/smell, dry mouth, brain fog, nausea, bad taste in the mouth, poor focus, insomnia, decreased physical performance, sore throat cramping, cravings, diarrhea, rapid heart rate, night sweats, poor focus, and muscle soreness.

These effects are the result of significant hormonal and metabolic changes.

What Happens?

Your body will have to re-learn about using fat as a source of energy as the muscle glycogen levels start dropping due to a lack of carbohydrate intake. It takes time for this "switch," and you feel low energy during that time, feel irritable and extreme cravings. How much you suffer will depend on how metabolically active you are.

As if that weren't enough, while your gallbladder and pancreas react to the extra fat intake, you may also notice gastrointestinal problems such as diarrhea.

Finally, the hormones will take a hit as your body re-balances minerals, fluids, and sources of energy. T3 and Cortisol, in particular. T3 is a thyroid hormone that depends on carbohydrates' ingestion to manage metabolism, and Cortisol would be a stress hormone.

What's the effective cure?

Many of the signs of adjusting to the carnivore diet can be minimized or even removed using a couple of easy tricks:

Eat more - the carnivore diet is naturally full of protein and high in fat, ensuring you can feel satisfied for a very long time. It could mean your daily intake of calories is much smaller. Find out how many calories you have to live and then consider when deciding on the amount of food.

Drink more - it's natural to drop a lot of fluids, particularly during the first few days, but if you don't want to experience the symptoms, these fluids need to be replaced.

Electrolytes - you can need more electrolytes if more water and food don't help. First, try to add some extra salt to your diet, but suggest an electrolyte supplement if you need to.

Sweat more - exercise is a perfect way to naturally eliminate excess contaminants and re-equalize the electrolyte levels.

Chapter 2: Breakfast Recipes for the Carnivore Diet

You may not have eaten for up to 10 hours when you wake up after your overnight sleep. Breakfast recharges the body's energy and nutrient reserves. In a brief period, it increases the energy levels and ability to focus and can decrease the risk of type 2 diabetes, long-term heart disease and improved weight management.

112.   1. Carnivore Breakfast Sandwich

It's delicious, easy, and rich in protein, fat, with no plants. This breakfast sandwich is appreciated by those on the carnivore diet or anyone who loves their diet with fat and protein. Although the Carnivore Breakfast Sandwich appears to criticize the mainstream cholesterol-preventing dietary advice, what we enjoy about this breakfast sandwich is how Incredibly delicious it is!

Prep Time: 5 Minutes

Cook Time: 5 Minutes

Total Time: 10 Minutes

Serving: 1

INGREDIENTS

- One egg
- One tsp bacon grease or butter.
- Two Sausage Patties beef
- 1-ounce cheddar cheese

INSTRUCTIONS

1. Melt butter on moderate temperature in a big skillet.
2. Shape the sausage into thin patties, about 1/2 inch thick but about the length of the palm. On the other side, cook patties until it turns to brown color, then flip, cook the other side for further 2-3 minutes, till then cooking continuously.
3. Fry an egg in the same pan at the same time. If not, in an additional pan (moderate temperature and take some time until the pan is hot to avoid sticking), use a little more butter and then prepare your carnivore breakfast sandwich. As with your sauce and keep sauce thin with yolk.
4. Set one sausage patty on a tray for preparation, then top it with a slice of cheese egg, another sausage patty, and top with a fried egg.
5. You can add sliced onion, sautéed spinach, or avocado as well. Enjoy the meal.

There's all in this Cheesy 3-Meat Breakfast Casserole recipe: sausage, plenty of cheese, bacon, and ham.   Perfect for a weekend breakfast or even during the holidays for visitors. A breakfast for lovers of meat!

Prep Time: 15 Minutes

Cook Time: 40 Minutes

Total Time: 55 Minutes

Servings: 10

Ingredients

- Seven ounces of ham chopped.

- Potatoes cut into cubes.

- 32 ounces chilled hash brown

- Two cups shredded cheddar cheese.

- Two cups of milk, eight large eggs, one tsp of salt.

- One medium onion (diced)

- Half teaspoon pepper.

- Twelve ounces breakfast sausage

- Twelve ounces bacon (diced into 1" pieces)

- Half tsp. garlic powder

Instructions

1. Spray with cooking spray on a 9x13" baking dish. Preheat oven to 350°F.

2. Cook the bacon pieces in a large non - stick frying pan once cooked thoroughly and become crispy. Don't overcook anymore. Remove the bacon from the bowl with a slotted spoon, leave the grease in the pan. Cook the sausage in the same frying pan over medium-high heat, breaking up the connections so that you have bite-sized bits (or smaller). When the sausage is roughly halfway finished, add the onion, and cook until the sausage is fully cooked. Stir the sausage/onion mixture into a bowl with a slotted spoon and leave the pan's grease.

3. After cooking both the bacon and the sausage and removing them from the pan, add the pan's brown hash potatoes. Cook the potatoes in the remaining grease over medium heat until they are softened and

browned slightly. In the lower part of the prepared baking dish, layer the hash browns.

4. Layer the cooked bacon on top of the hash browns, the ham, and the sausage/onion mixture. Then, scatter the cheese equally over the beef.

5. Whisk the eggs with the milk, garlic powder, salt, and pepper together in a big cup. On the upper side of the covered ingredients of the baking dish, add the egg mixture on top.

6. Bake for about 35-40 minutes in the oven or until the egg is fully set and the cheese is soft and bubbly.

114.   3. One-Pan Egg and Turkey Skillet Recipe

You now need to have this One-Pan Egg and Turkey Skillet if you are looking for an easy, nutritious, and delicious meal. You're going to love that. The most important meal of the day is breakfast. So, with this balanced breakfast, start your day right off.

Prep Time: 5 Minutes

Cook Time: 20 Minutes

Total Time: 25 Minutes

Servings: 6

INGREDIENTS

- Six eggs

- One cup salsa

- Pepper and salt according to taste.

- 1 pound ground turkey

INSTRUCTIONS

1. Spray with non-stick cooking spray on the skillet and add in ground turkey.

2. Cook until the turkey is golden brown, over moderate flame. Also, drain all grease.

3. Connect the salsa mixture and blend well. For 2-3 minutes, cook the turkey and salsa.

4. Put the eggs in the skillet and cover them for 7 to 9 minutes or until the eggs are cooked to your taste.

115.   4. Keto and Carnivore Meatloaf Muffin

It's quick to make this amazing Keto and Carnivore Meatloaf Muffin Meal, tasty but without all the fillers and perfect for taking for work or breakfast on-the-go. You can keep them all week long to eat in advance.

Prep Time: 15 Minutes

Cook Time: 25 Minutes

Servings: 2

Ingredients

- Two eggs

- 2 lbs. 85 percent ground beef

- Two tsps. Sea salt.

Optional Ingredients:

- Two tsps. paprika

- No-sugar added ketchup for topping.

- One tbsp. garlic powder

- Half tsp. black powder

Instructions

1. To 350 degrees, set the oven.
2. Mix the eggs, meat, spices, and salt, if used, in a large mixing bowl with both hands until well mixed.
3. Using the liners to prepare the muffin pan.
4. Use meat to fill each cup until it is three times the amount filled.
5. Put the muffins in the oven with the meatloaf and put it in the oven for 25-35 minutes.
6. Muffins can cook quicker or slower, based on your oven.
7. Check a muffin by gently cut the hot muffin in half after about 20 minutes.
8. Take the muffin pan from the oven. If it seems done enough in your taste, present the muffins with tongs, and eat.

116. 5. Carnivore Keto Burgers

If you are considering the Carnivore diet, these burgers will become one of your favorite meals. You get enough calories from this to keep your energy up, so fattier meat cuts are best.

Prep Time: 5 Minutes

Cook Time: 10 Minutes

Total Time: 15 Minutes

Servings: 8

Ingredients

- One teaspoon salt.

- 200 grams Speck or bacon 0.5 pound

- 500 grams Ground Beef (Beef grind) 1 pound

- 500 grams Ground Pork (Pork grind) 1 pound

- Two tablespoons Southwest Seasoning

Instructions

1. Cut the speck to the smallest possible size. If you want everything chopped/ground more equally, you can also use a mincer or food processor.

2. Combine it in a large bowl with all the items.

3. Generally, divide the mixture into eight patties and shape each by hand into a patty style.

4. BBQ on high/heat grill

5. Switch the grill/Barbeque down to low and put patties and straighten with a spatula on the grill/BBQ.

6. Please enable it to cook for 5 minutes on the grill, then flipped and cook for another five min. It is going to make the burgers well done.

7. Add and display your favorite seasonings.

117. 6 Low-carb baked eggs

A great low-carb combination of eggs and beef. Please, yes! At any moment, cook up this delicious gem-lunch, dinner, or breakfast. You will be thanked by your every taste buds!

Prep Time: 5 Minutes

Cook Time: 10 Minutes.

Serving: 1

Ingredients

- Two eggs

- Half cup (2 oz.) grated cheese

- Three oz. Ground turkey or ground pork or ground beef cook it any way you like.

Instructions

1. Heat the oven to 200 °C (400 °F).
2. Arrange a cooked mixture of ground beef in a little baking dish. Then, using a spoon, make two holes and crack the eggs into them.
3. Sprinkle the end with shredded cheese.
4. Cook in the oven for around 10-15 minutes, till the eggs are cooked.
5. Allow it to cool for a little while. The ground meat and eggs get very hot.

Tip for the recipe

- It is a great recipe for the remaining hamburger you weren't sure what to do. Accumulate the recipe by the number of people and the entire family; you'll have dinner. Tada!

- Complement this with fresh herbs and avocado with quite a crunchy, crisp salad. Or give this a try with this amazing homemade mayonnaise (made without additives and soybean oil).

A delicious recipe eaten for lunch, breakfast, or dinner is this easy Spam and Eggs. These cheesy meat eggs in less than fifteen min make a perfect, fast breakfast!

Prep Time: 5 Minutes.

Cook Time: 10 Minutes.

Total Time: 15 Minutes

Servings: 2

Ingredients

- Two eggs are well beaten.

- Two ounces Cheddar cheese, shredded.

- One (12 ounces) bowl of fully cooked luncheon meat (for example, spam) cut into cubes.

Instructions

Under moderate heat on a non-stick pan, put the eggs in, then spam. Cooked and stir till the eggs are almost ready, then spread over the cheese and mix until it is melted.

Chapter 3: Lunch Recipes for Carnivore Diet

The lunch hour helps your brain to relax, refresh, and remain focused, although it will directly increase your productivity for the rest of the day. Taking some time out during the day, yet if you choose to take some brief breaks, offers your brain an opportunity to recharge. Getting the proper ratio of meals is the secret to a balanced packed lunch to give you the nutrition you have to remain healthy.

119.   1. Carnivore Chicken Nuggets

Everyone enjoys chicken nuggets. This beautiful and tasty recipe is simple and full of nutrients to develop. Appreciate the meals which everyone enjoys in a healthily!

Prep Time: 40 minutes

Cook Time: 20 minutes

 Servings: 60 nuggets.

Ingredients

- One large egg

- Mixture of bread

- half teaspoon oregano

- One cup of parmesan cheese is shredded.

- One cup pork rinds ground

- Three lbs. ground chicken or chop your own.

- Chicken Mixture

- half teaspoon pink salt

Instructions

1. Preheat the oven to 400°C.

2. Step cookie sheet with baking paper.

3. In a flat pan, merge the cheese and ground pork.

4. Stir up your egg, spices, and chicken.

5. From the chicken mixture, shape a small patty of the size you want. On the breading, put the mixture.

6. Cover the chicken with the mixture using a fork.

7. Place it on a cookie sheet lined with parchment.

8. Please continue with steps 5 - 7 till you have used all the chicken. If you are out of bread, make more of it.

9. Bake for 20 minutes at 400 degrees.

120. 2. Cheesy Air Fryer Meatballs

You can make tasty, healthy meatballs in even less than thirty min, without any greasy mess! Real easy low carb meal in your air fryer for Cheesy Meatballs made fast and easy. Perfect for those who are on the carnivore diet.

Prep Time: 20 Minutes

Cook Time: 12 Minutes

Resting Time: 8 Minutes

Total Time: 40 Minutes

Servings: 6 (4 meat-balls servings)

Equipment

Air Fryer

Ingredients

- One tablespoon lard

- 2 ounces pork rinds

- Three ounces shredded Italian cheese blend.

- One teaspoon pink sea salt

- Two pounds grass-fed ground beef

- Two large, well-blended eggs

Instructions

1. In a mixing bowl, add all of the items. Mash the mixture with clean hands till it is fully mixed.

2. Roll around 1 1/2 inches in diameter into balls. Twenty-four meatballs will be prepared by this method.

3. You'll cook them in parts, which vary according to the size of your air fryer.

4. If you use them, fill your fryer basket with liners. Otherwise, spray with cooking spray.

5. Put meatballs in the basket, ensuring they do not touch the basket's sides and each other.

6. Cook for 8 minutes at 350 degrees. Bring the basket out and switch over the balls of meat. Return to the frying pan and cook for another 4 minutes at 350 degrees.

7. The core temperature of the meatballs should approach 165 degrees, and then they're cooked!

3. Scallops with Wrapped Bacon

Jumbo scallops covered in a flavorful glaze are the bacon-wrapped scallops and broiled to satisfaction. A quick but tasteful appetizer and the main course choice that will get rave reviews for sure!

Prep Time: 20 minutes

Cook Time: 15 minutes

Total Time: 35 minutes

Servings: 6

INGREDIENTS

- One-pound bacon slices diced in the half crossway.

- Two tablespoons of well-diced parsley.

- Two tablespoons soy sauce

- Pepper and salt according to your taste,

- 2 pounds large sea scallops patted dry.

- A cup of quarter fourth maple syrup

- 1/4 teaspoon garlic powder and

- cooking spray

INSTRUCTIONS

1. Preheat your broiler. Utilizing cooking spray to cover a sheet pan.
2. Cover each scallop around a slice of bacon and fix it with a toothpick. Put the scallops on the baking pan in a single layer.
3. Whisk all together soy sauce, pepper, salt, garlic powder and maple syrup in a small cup. Brush from over the top from each of the scallops with half the paste.
4. Broil around 10-15 minutes, just until the bacon becomes crispy and cooked through scallops. Half the way through the cooking process, brush the leftover sauce and over scallops.
5. Sprinkle parsley and serve.

122.   4. Steak Tartare

If you are on the carnivore diet and love healthy, fresh flavors, this homemade Steak Tartare (or Beef Tartare) is something you can make at home.

Total Time: 30 minutes (includes freezing time)

Active Time: 25 minutes

Servings: 4

Ingredients:

- Two large egg yolks

- Six tbsps. finely diced shallots

- One tsp. kosher salt

- Half tsp. dry mustard

- Two tsps. sherry vinegar

- Sixteen ounces top sirloin cleaned and trimmed.

- 2 tbsps. Fresh parsley is finely diced and divided.

- One tsp. freshly grated lemon zest

- 1/4 cup celery leaves are finely diced and divided.

- 1/4 cup light olive oil

- Two tbsps. Small brined capers drained and unrinsed.

Instructions

1. Custom instruments: pastry ring 3 3/4-inch, food processor (optional)

2. Slice the steak into 1-inch pieces and set aside for 10 mins in the refrigerator.

3. In a small bowl, mix dry mustard, egg yolks, and vinegar. Stir continuously until caramelized while streaming in the oil, then whisk in the salt, shallots, capers, parsley, and around 2/3 of the celery leaves.

4. Cut the meat to your preferred shape through the hand. (Likewise, distribute the meat in 4 quantities and pulse each batch in the food processor bowl fitted with the regular S-blade 3 to 4 times separately.)

5. With neat hands, bend the meat and flavor it easily. Plate and garnish with the lemon zest and reserved herbs using a 3 3/4-inch pastry ring.

123. 5. Low-Carb Beef Bourguignon Stew

It is likely to obtain this dish of Low-Carb Beef Bourguignon Stew in an Instant Pot or slow cooker. It can be enjoyed by those on Atkins, low carb, keto, diabetics, gluten-free, Paleo, grain-free, or Banting Diet.

Prep Time: 30 minutes

Cook Time: 30 minutes

Total Time: 1 hour

Servings: 6

Ingredients

- Four ounces white onion (about 1 small)

- Two stalks celery sliced.

- Eight ounces of mushrooms thickly cut into pieces.

- 1 1/2-pound stew meat diced into 1 1/2 -2-inch cubes and dry with a paper towel.

- Four pieces of bacon cut crosswise.

- 1/4 tsp. Black pepper freshly ground.

- 1/2 tsp. sea salt (or to taste)

- 1 cup dry burgundy wine

- 1/2 tsp. dried thyme

- 1 tbsp. Fresh parsley chopped.

- One clove of garlic crushed.

- Half tsp. Xanthan gum.

- One cup beef stock or, you can use low-salt broth.

- Two tbsps. tomato paste

- One bay leaf

Instructions

Instant Pot instructions

1. As the Instant Pot covers off, select the sauté mode. Add the bacon when the "hot" sign appears. Cook the bacon till crispy, mixing frequently. Remove it to a plate lined with paper towels. Do not remove grease comprising bacon.

2. To an Instant Kettle, add half of the beef. Use the pepper and salt to sprinkle. Before flipping, make the first side brown. Brown both ends of it and pull it to a tray. For the other half of the beef, repeat. If during this process, the Instant Pot switches off, set again to Sauté.

3. Discharge of all but one tablespoon of the pot's drippings. (Add around a tablespoon of recommended oil or butter to the Instant

Pot if there is less than one tablespoon) Continue with the sauté setting and add the celery and onion to the pot. Please enable it to cook until it starts to soften. Add the mushrooms. Cook the vegetables until they begin to soften the mushrooms. Stir in the garlic and cook for a moment. Transfer to a dish.

4. Add about a teaspoon if there's no oil left in the pot. To the pot, add the xanthan gum. Stir through the xanthan gum to spread the oil. Pour the burgundy in and mix, scraping the brown pieces together. Simmer until the wine begins to thicken. Add broth of beef. Whisk in the tomato paste, thyme, and bay leaf. Just take it to a simmer. Enable to boil until the broth thickens enough for a spoon to stick. Send browned chunks of beef (including the drippings) and bacon to the pot of vegetables. Stir in the salt and pepper.

5. Cover Instant Pot. "Steam release location handle for "Sealing." To change the time to 30 minutes, select the Meat/Stew feature and press the +/- button. Used this Quick Release method (follow Instant Pot instruction book) to vent the Instant Pot when the stew is finished. Press Cancel. When opening the lid, be sure the float valve is down.

6. Taste the seasoning and adjust. Until serving, cut the bay leaf and sprinkle it with parsley.

Slow cooker instructions:

(add 5 hours and 30 minutes to cooking time)

1. On moderate flame, heat the Dutch oven or large soup pot. Add the bacon when the pot is hot. Cook the bacon till crisp, stirring occasionally. Lift to a plate lined with paper towels to clean and transfer to the slow cooker.

2. To the pot, put 1/2 of the beef. Chunks shouldn't harm you. Using pepper and salt to sprinkle. Before flipping, cause the first side to brown. Then brown flip both sides to the slow cooker. For the other part of the meat, return.

3. Discharge of all but 1 tbsp of the pot's drippings. If less than a tablespoon is available, add a little of the oil of your choice. Cl Continue to add the celery and onions to the pot over moderate temperature. Please enable it to cook till it starts to soften. Add the mushrooms. Cook the vegetables until they begin to soften the mushrooms. Stir in the garlic and boil for a minute. Place the vegetables in a crockpot.

4. Add about a teaspoon of your oil choice if there is no oil left in the tank. To the jar, add the xanthan gum. Stir in the oil to spread it. Pour the burgundy in and stir, scraping the brown bits together. Simmer and simmer until the wine begins to thicken. Add broth of beef. Stir in the tomato paste, bay leaf, and thyme. Just bring it to a simmer. Enable to boil until the broth thickens enough for a spoon to coat. Stir in the pepper and salt. Shift the bacon, beef, and vegetables to the slow cooker and mix.

5. Then seal the slow cooker. Process the stew for six-eight hours or until meat is cooked.

6. Taste and change the seasoning when served. Before serving, extract the bay leaf and sprinkle it with parsley.

Lunch Meat Roll-Ups seem to be simple to create, adaptable enough to suit everyone's different interests, and make an ideal keto lunch or healthy meal! As specific and over the edge as you prefer, you can also make these roll-ups!

Prep Time: 5 minutes

Total Time: 5 minutes

Servings: 2

Ingredients

- Four pieces of cheese

- Four pieces of lunch meat

- garnishes of your preference if you want shredded lettuce, herb cream cheese, guacamole.

- black pepper and sea salt

Instructions

1. On the workplace surface, put your meat pieces and garnish them with a cheese slice.
2. Note: This would be a wonderful time to guacamole or dressings of your choice on top, herb spread cream cheese,
3. Wrap your lunch meat across the cheese till you have a log, starting from the bottom.
4. Continue to roll up your rolls of meat and cheese until you reach the amount you would like. Use black pepper and sea salt to sprinkle.
5. Serve with a leafy green salad or bowl of bone broth.

Note

Please press on your lunch meat's thicker side to be cut to be smoother to roll and remain together.

7. Carnivore Braised Beef Shank

It's a highly versatile recipe that can be made from a cast-iron skillet or Dutch oven to a crockpot to an instant pot with multiple cooking equipment. You can also slow-cook it in the oven rather than cooking on the stovetop. You get a delicious lunchtime recipe!

Prep Time: 5 Minutes

Cook Time: 3 hrs.

Total Time: 3 hrs. 5 mins

Servings: 4

EQUIPMENT

Cast iron skillet.

Dutch oven

INGREDIENTS

- Two-three cups of bone broth or water

- One tbsp ghee, beef tallow butter or other cooking fat.

- Four pieces beef shank 1-inch thick, eight ounces each

- One tsp. Salt or as you required.

INSTRUCTIONS

1. In the Dutch oven or cast iron or heavy bottom skillet with cover, burn the cooking fat. Brown from both sides of the beef shanks till a golden-brown crust forms, about 2-3 minutes each side.

2. Over shanks, pour the broth. Use 2 cups of broth, at least. The considerable broth will be acceptable 1/2 to 3/4 of the way up the side to cover the meat, with salt, season. Bring a boil to it.

3. Reduce heat and cover the pot and let the steam escape from a tiny hole.

4. Cook for 3 hours, over a low flame, till the meat begins to fall off the bone. Serve warm in liquid.

NOTES

- Over the last 30 minutes of the cooking process, add any of the vegetables and herbs mentioned above and cook with the meat.

- Oven method Follow steps 1-2, then place the lid on after broth is simmering and switch to the oven for 2 hours for the roast.

- Crockpot Method put meat in a slow cooker's bottom, pour broth over and sprinkle with salt. Cover it with your cover and turn it down. Cooked for 4-6 hours before the bone breaks down easily.

- Seasoning the meat with the instant pot method. Turn the Instant pot on and choose to sauté. When heated, add the cooking fat to the pot and cook the meat until golden brown, around 2-3 minutes on each side. Add some broth. Close the sealing valve and lid. Put the high pressure in order and cook for 35 minutes. For 15 minutes, the normal release pressure releases the remaining pressure gradually.

125.   8. Herb Roasted Bone Marrow

Marrow is an outstanding substitute of the omega-3s essential for safe brain growth and anti-inflammation. It's very, very beneficial for everyone.

It's fairly affordable if you prepare it straight away (versus having it at a fine dining restaurant). It's incredibly tasty.

Prep time: 5 mins

Cook time: 15 mins.

Total time: 20 mins

Servings: 1-2 marrow bones

INGREDIENTS

- Fresh rosemary

- Marrow bones from grass-fed/pasture-raised beef, 1-2 each person

- black pepper and salt

- Fresh thyme

INSTRUCTIONS

1. For one person, the marrow with one or two pieces of bone is quite enough.

2. Defrost it properly if the bones are frozen.

3. To 400 degrees, set the oven. In a baking dish, put the bones. Spacing does not matter - closely or loosely, it is spaced.

4. Finely chop the thyme and fresh rosemary into equal parts. Use 1/2 teaspoon of chopped herbs for four marrow bones. Over the marrow bones, sprinkle the spices.

5. Roast for around fifteen min, until the inside is no longer pink. Until the marrow starts to "cook out" of the bones, you had to catch them.

6. Serve hot and season with salt and pepper. Scoop out the marrow using a spoon.

7. Save any drippings in an airtight jar in the refrigerator for a few days, as well as the remaining marrow. Chop the leftover marrow finely and toss it for a flavor and nutrient boost with hot, cooked vegetables.

Chapter 4: Desserts and Snack Recipes for the Carnivore Diet

After all, it's all about satisfying the soul with food for dessert enthusiasts that allows them to realize like they've reached Paradise on earth at last. Eating dessert does not indicate that you have little or no control over yourself. It just means you've got a clear idea of what you want (it's just a delicious blueberry cheesecake sometimes), and you've got what it takes to satisfy these cravings.

126.   1. Bacony Carnivore Womelletes

This one is excellent topped with cinnamon butter as well as a pour of pancake syrup without sugar. For sandwiches, it also stands up very well.

Prep Time: 2 minutes

Cook Time: 8 minutes

Total Time: 10 minutes

Servings: 2 womelletes.

INGREDIENTS

- One large egg.

- One slice of bacon (raw)

- hefty pinch of any spices or flavorings as you want.

- Splash maple extract, if required.

INSTRUCTIONS

1. Put the bacon in a food processor or blender and turn it on.

2. Put any seasonings and egg down the chute until the bacon is ground up and start operating the machine till liquified and well-in incorporated. It is your womelletes slurry.

3. As per its directions, warm your mini-waffle machine.

4. In a waffle maker, add half the slurry and place the cover around.

5. Cook for around 3-5 mins max till golden or to your preferred level of flavor and texture.

6. Take away from the waffle maker, and with the leftover slurry, repeat the procedure 4 and 5.

7. Enjoy the womelletes warm or as you are delighted.

127. 2. Carnivore Cake

While you follow the carnivore diet strictly and sometimes seem to desire a dessert, well, we have nothing sweet for you, but we've got a cake.

Prep Time: 5 minutes

Cook Time: 10 minutes

Total Time: 25 minutes

Servings: 8

INGREDIENTS

- Seven oz creamy cheese

- One pinch of dill for decoration

- Ten oz smoked salmon

- Eight eggs

- One pinch salt

INSTRUCTIONS

1. Inside a small bowl, beat the salt and eggs until mixed.

2. Heat skillet or 6-in nonstick pan over the moderate flame while heated.

3. To coat the pan's base, pour 1/4 cup of the mixture into the pan and whisk. Adjust the pan to the flame and allow the eggs to cook.

4. Cooked the egg crepes till they are just set (about 30 seconds) on the bottom, so there is no browning on the sides. Turn gently over the crepe and cook on the opposite side for a couple of seconds.

5. Repeat till all the mixture is used.

6. To cool off, place the cooking crepes on a wire rack or a plate.

Let us bring everything together.

- Bring one crepe upon this plate and cover it with a thin coating of cream cheese.

- Layer cream cheese with diced smoked salmon and top with next crepe.

- Continue layering till all components are being used.

- Customize and serve with dill.

NOTE:

In the refrigerator, let the cake stay for 1 hour; it'll be smoother to break. For decorative purposes, utilize fresh dill.

3. Egg Custard

With its elegant yet mild taste and its creaminess, this traditional dessert is still a highlight. Preferably sized for a children's treat yet mature enough for a formal dinner, it requires just 15 minutes to prepare and can be kept for up to 3 days in the fridge, sealed. (The evening once you've made this is much better.)

Prep Time: 10 minutes

Cook Time: 2 hours.

Servings: 6

INGREDIENTS

- Two eggs
- Two cups whole milk
- Two egg yolks

- 1/3 cup sugar

- Freshly shredded or ground nutmeg

- One tsp. of vanilla extract

PREPARATION

1. Heat the oven around 300 degrees.

2. Placed in a deep baking pan broad enough to accommodate six 4-ounce ovenproof cups (you can use coffee cups or ramekins marked as oven-safe).

3. Get the milk to a boil with moderate flame in a medium-size saucepan.

4. In the meantime, mix the yolks, sugar, vanilla, and eggs in a distinct dish.

5. Through boiling milk, stir the egg mixture, stirring gently to incorporate.

6. Pour the mixture into the cups via a fine strainer (unless the strainer clogs, choose a spoon to scrape it clean), then drizzled with the nutmeg gently.

7. In the pan, pour hot (not boiling) water till it hits half the way up the cups' ends.

8. Bake for 30 to 35 minutes until the custard is just finished (it can still be a bit loose).

9. Before served, just let the custard cool in cold water for around 2 hours.

4. Carnivore Chaffle Recipe

Because of the sauce, this meal has only one net carb. With a small salad aside, it can be served. It is very satisfying and tastes delicious! 1 serving in the oven renders this recipe.

Prep Time: 3 minutes

Cook Time: 8 minutes

Serving: 1

INGREDIENTS

- 1/4 cup parmesan cheese shredded.

- 1/4 cup chopped pork rinds.

- One egg is well beaten.

- One tsp. Grill mate roasted garlic and herb flavoring.

INSTRUCTIONS

1. In a small bowl, mix all the ingredients and incorporate until thoroughly mixed.

2. Cover it with a silicone sheet or parchment paper using a small baking sheet.

3. Through wet hands, tap the mixture into a small circle or use a silicone spatula to create the pizza crust.

4. The oven baking duration is bake around each side for 10 minutes at 350 degrees in the oven.

5. Mini Dash Waffle Maker: Split the mixture into two and cook every other serving for at least 4 minutes before a crust forms (it could take longer if you are using a large waffle iron)

6. Air Fryer Baking Time: Cook on each side at 300 degrees for eight minutes.

7. If you prefer to remove the carnivore pizza crust with any seasonings and place the keto-friendly sauce of choice on. Mostly prefer black olives and Italian sausage.

8. Place 1/3 of mozzarella cheese on top.

9. Place the cheese in the oven, air fryer, or microwave until it becomes crispy, just long enough to melt. It takes just 1 minute for the microwave or 3 to 4 minutes for the oven or air fryer.

A meat bagel is meat that has been molded into a bagel pattern and served like a bagel. For the keto, Paleo, low carb, and for those on the carnivore diet, it is the ideal bagel!

Prep Time: 15 minutes

Cook Time: 40 minutes

Total Time: 55 minutes

Serving: 6

INGREDIENTS

- Two pounds ground pork

- 2/3 cup of tomato sauce

- Two large eggs

- 1 ½ onion, finely diced.

- 1/2 tsp ground pepper

- One tablespoon butter/bacon/ grass-fed ghee fat etc.

- One teaspoon sea salt

- One teaspoon paprika

INSTRUCTIONS

1. Heat the oven to 400°F. Create a parchment paper baking dish.

2. Sauté the onions with some cooking fat over a moderate flame, like grass-fed ghee butter etc. Sauté once they're transparent. Before placing them in the meat, allow the onions to chill.

3. Adjust all the components in a dish, along with the fried onions. Blend enough to disperse the spices uniformly.

4. Distribute the meat into six pieces. Roll a piece into a ball utilizing the hands, shape the center, and straighten gently to create a bagel.

5. Put the meat-looking bagel in the dish and proceed with each of the meat parts.

6. Bake until the meat is completely cooked, or for 40 minutes.

7. Enable the cooling of the meat bagels. Just like a normal bagel, slice the meat bagel. Load the meat bagel with salads such as slices of onions, tomato, spinach, etc.

Chapter 5: Dinner Recipes for the Carnivore Diet

Dinner is also an essential meal, and with a variety of amazing foods, you can try new things. Better sleep, greater stress resilience, reduced inflammation, lower anxiety, improved digestion, and steady sugar levels are connected to a nutritious meal.

129.   1. Pot Roast Recipe with Gravy

Without lots of vegetables such as onions and garlic, you think you can't make Carnivore Diet Pot Roast because you are on the carnivore diet and can't consume vegetables. Here is the recipe, which is full of nutrition and quite easy to make.

Prep Time: 10 minutes

Cook Time: 3 hours.

Servings: 4

Ingredients

- 1 4-5- lbs. pot roast

- Four thsps. Butter or ghee.

- Two tsps. Sea salt.

- Three to Six cups of beef broth

Instructions

Recipe Notes

Cooking Time:

90 minutes Instant Pot

7 hours Slow Cooker

Stove Top

1. Heat the oven to 325°C. On both sides, salt the roast. On moderate temperature, heat the heavy bottom pan with a cover and put two tbsp of ghee.

2. Once the pan seems to be very hot, brown both sides of the roast from the surface for around 1-2 minutes.

3. From each side, whenever the pot roast is cooked, add the broth till the pot roast is coated and Put the cover and cook in the oven.

4. Bake in the oven for 2-3 hours, while enclosed, till it is fork-tender. Take it out of the oven and set off.

5. On moderate flame, place a small saucepan, add 1.5 cups of the remaining broth and the leftover 2 tbsp of ghee.

6. For 5-6 minutes, whisk the saucepan constantly till the broth decreases and thickens.

7. On a large dish, put the slice and roast crosswise. On over pot roast, put the thickened sauce.

8. Start serving and have a pleasant time.

Instant Pot

1. Turn on the device to sauté mode and dissolve the ghee.

2. For around two min each, add the pot roast and cook it on every side.

3. When the meat is wrapped, add the broth, and fix the cover, ensuring that the vent is covered.

4. Cooked for 90 minutes over high temperature.

5. Let the pressure automatically escape and ensure that it is a fork-tender.

6. Under moderate flame, put a small saucepan and pour 1.5 cups of the Instant Pot's remaining broth and two leftover tbsp of ghee.

7. For 5-6 mins, whisk the saucepan constantly till the broth decreases and thickens.

8. In the representing tray, move the pot roast and cut it crosswise.

9. Over the pot roast, spill the sauce. Start Serving and enjoy the meal.

Slow Cooker

1. Heat the frying pan on moderately high heat and dissolve the ghee.

2. Put the pot roast and cook it for about 2 minutes on every side till it is browned.

3. To the slow cooker, add the roast and add in the broth till it covers the meat.

4. About 6 hours, cooked on high heat as well as the meat is fork-tender.

5. Add 1.5 cups of broth and the leftover two tablespoons of ghee to a medium saucepan at moderate temperature.

6. For 3-5 minutes, stir the saucepan constantly until the broth decreases and thickens.

7. Move the pot roast to a serving dish and slice it crosswise into pieces.

8. On over pot roast, spill the thickened sauce. Present the meal and enjoy.

A quick and simple Carnivore Skillet Pepperoni Pizza will fulfill the desire for pizza! Also, when you are on the Carnivore diet, no need to skip family pizza evening. One pan and just a couple of supplies!

Prep Time: 10 Minutes

Cook Time: 15 Minutes

Total Time: 25 Minutes

Servings: 4

Ingredients

- 2 oz (1/2 cup) mozzarella cheese, grated.

- Four eggs.

- Pizza Base.

- Two tablespoon mayonnaise or melted butter, tallow, or lard.

- Pepperoni slices to cover the pizza.

- One tsp each garlic and onion powder.

- Pinch of salt for the taste.

- One teaspoon Italian seasoning.

- More Italian seasoning you can use if you need it.

- More cheese to sprinkle on top as you want it.

- Pizza Topping.

- 2 oz shredded parmesan.

Instructions

1. Heat the oven around 375°C.

2. Oil the cast iron frying pan.

3. Mix the cheese, eggs, seasoning and 2tbsp fat, all ingredients in a dish.

4. Into cast iron pan, add the mixture.

5. Sprinkle with some flavorings, cheese, and pepperoni on top.

6. Cook for 15 minutes in the oven or till the pizza is swollen and the layer starts to brown.

7. Slice it into four parts and try it!

3. Carnivore Ham and Cheese Noodle Soup

A Carnivore diet noodle recipe!? Cheese, bacon, bone broth, ham and fresh carnivore noodles are mixed in this rich cheesy, comforting nutritional soup! A pleasant change of style of the regular entry for the carnivore diet!

Prep Time: 15 Minutes

Cook Time: 15 Minutes

Total Time: 30 Minutes

Servings: 4

Ingredients

- 2 oz cream cheese cut into small pieces.

- 10-12 oz cubed cooked ham

- 1/4 cup bacon chopped or 3-4 pieces of cooked crisp bacon finely diced

- Two cups of bone broth or regular broth

- One cup Carnivore Noodles if you want it.

- Two cups cheddar cheese, shredded (save 1/2 cup for garnish)

- half cup heavy cream

- Pepper and Salt according to your taste.

Instructions

1. Heat the broth in a large medium pot until it almost begins to boil. Hold the broth at a reasonable volume.

2. Mix in the cubes of cream cheese and whisk until the broth is mixed and the chunks are removed.

3. Whisk in the finely chopped cheese till it mixes into the combination, about half a cup at a time.

4. Add the noodles and cubed ham and bring to a boil until fully cooked.

5. Mix in heavy cream and boil for a further min on low flame.

6. Cover each bowl with crumbled or chopped bacon and saved shredded cheddar cheese. Split into four wide bowls.

4. Carnivore Moussaka

It is a high-calorie meal, especially when it comes to high-fat sheep yogurt, aged cheese, and butter. In contrast, please remember that the only thing that contributes carbohydrates to this meal is sheep yogurt. Suppose when it falls to the taste. Just try this recipe because it can satisfy your tastebuds.

Prep Time: 30 minutes

Cooking Time: 40 minutes

Servings: 4

INGREDIENTS

- 250g (8,8 oz) chopped lamb.

- 250g (8.8 oz) diced beef or veal.

- Eight medium eggs

- 400g (14 oz) Sheep yogurt – strained Greek type (As a substitute use sour cream)

- 500g (1 Lb.) thin veal cutlets

- 50g (1,7 oz) butter or ghee (we always use sheep or goat butter)

- 100g shredded kefalograviera cheese

Spice mixture (amounts to your liking)

- powder rosemary

- dry oregano

- red, white, and black pepper freshly ground.

- dry peppermint

- smoked red paprika powder.

- Ceylon cinnamon

- garlic powder

- sea salt

- ground bay leaves

Instructions

1. Get your chopped meat layer prepared first. In a saucepan or deep-frying pan, dissolve the butter and brown your meat paste in it. Put all the seasoning, except for the oregano, from the list to your taste. In the final moment, you can put oregano so that it does not get sour. Take from heat once the meat sauce is prepared and add one egg. Stir rapidly. Set it down.

2. Roll the veal cutlets with either a sliding pin Grease some butter or ghee to ceramic baking dish or clay.

3. Using a pinch of pepper and sea salt to mix one egg. Dip the egg into each veal slice and put that on the base of the baking dish.

4. Bake at 180oC (350oF) for 10 minutes in the oven.

5. Mix the sheep yogurt or sour cream with six eggs use an electric blender. To your taste, add a pinch of salt.

6. Put the meat sauce over the veal's slices and put the Carnivore moussaka back in the oven. Around ten min, bake. Then coat it with the paste of yogurt or cream and eggs and move it to the oven. Proceed to bake for the next 10 minutes.

7. Then coat it with finely chopped Kefalograviera cheese and layer it uniformly. Please put it back in the oven and cook for ten more minutes. By switching on just the upper heater in the oven, you may use the top process roasting.

8. Represent with a little more finely chopped cheese or a little bit more sour cream. Using fresh parsley or some other texture.

NOTES

You can only use chopped meat sauce for a slightly quicker recipe and cover it with cheese and fluffy topping.

Do not slice till it has cool down at least half the way. It will help you to slice sharp sides with neat pieces.

5. AIP Chicken Bacon Sauté

A delight for the Carnivore's diet: These

AIP chicken bacon sautés indeed a tasty dish that gratifies and best serves you.

Prep Time: 10 minutes

Cook Time: 20 minutes

Servings: 2

INGREDIENTS

- Four pieces of bacon, diced.

- One tbsp. garlic powder

- One tbsp avocado oil for cooking

- One chicken breast small diced.

- Salt according to taste.

- 2 tbsps. Italian seasoning

INSTRUCTIONS

1. In a frying pan, add the avocado oil and cook the bacon and chicken. Cooked for approximately 10 min.

2. For seasoning, use Italian seasoning, garlic powder and salt according to your taste.

Point to note All nutrition information is calculated and concentrated on quantities per serving.

131.   6. Low Carb Carnitas

Cooked at home carnitas enjoyed with freshly chopped avocados and crunchy onions a quick low carb meal, but it can be a meal memory pretty fast! It is indeed chosen easily to low-carb lifestyle choices, and this carnitas is so delicious that tortillas ought not to be missed in the end.

Prep Time: 30 minutes

Cook Time: 2 hrs. 15 minutes.

Servings: 10

Ingredients

- 3 lb. boneless pork shoulder roast cut into 1–2-inch pieces.

- Four sprigs of fresh thyme

- Two cups of water.

- Half cup finely diced onion.

- One teaspoon chipotle spice chooses the spice that suits your taste.

- One orange.

- Prefer one tablespoon lard or oil.

- Two tablespoon lard olive oil if you don't want lard.

- Two bay leaves, one teaspoon dry oregano

- One teaspoon salt.

- Three cloves garlic finely diced.

Instructions

1. Take the orange and then suck the orange juice out of it. In a bowl, bring it together and put it aside.

2. Heat 2 tablespoons of lard above medium-high heat in a heavy bottom pot or large Dutch oven. To line the pot's base, put some sliced meat in one layer, be careful not to create a mess. Cook the first layer of meat till it is browned, flipping both sides brown using tongs. Transfer to a plate if that meat layer is

browned and apply the new layer of meat and cook till browned, then switch to the plate. Rinse until all the meat is browned, then modify.

3. Add the garlic and onion to the Dutch oven pot when the meat is browned, then take away from the pan. Cooked for about 5 minutes or so, frequently mixing, till the onions are crispy and crunchy. Getting back to meat.

4. Utilize the preserved orange zest and juice to the Dutch oven and the next six ingredients (through the Chile pepper). Take it to a boil, lower the heat and cover it. For 2 hours, boil.

5. Take the pot back to a gentle simmer after 2 hours and cook disclosed for 15 to 20 minutes or until most of the liquid has vanished, moving constantly. Take away the bay leaves and thyme sprigs and go to the next stage or store the meat till it is ready. The meat can be stored in the fridge for up to 3 days at this stage.

6. Heat One Tablespoon of lard over the moderate temperature in a big skillet while cooking the carnitas. Remove the meat from the sauce using a slotted spoon and place it over a thin line in the skillet. Cooked for five min or till the meat begins to crust, slightly flipping (you may need to do this in batches).

7. Offer with lime wedges, guacamole (or sliced fresh avocados), refried beans, jalapeno pepper, lime wedges, and caramelized onions.

132.   7. Carnivore's Lasagna

For meat lovers, it is stuffed with Italian sausage, ground beef, meatballs, and pepperoni.

Prep Time: 1 hour 10 minutes.

Cook Time: 1 hour.

Servings: 1 lasagna

INGREDIENTS

- Half onion finely chopped.

- 1 lb. hot Italian sausage sliced.

- Four garlic cloves crumbled.

- 1 1/2 cups parmesan cheese, grated.

- One tsp. Dry oregano, divided.

- 1/2 cup oatmeal

- 3 (15 ounce) cans tomato sauce

- 2 tbsps. Brown sugar

- 18 lasagna noodles

- One tbsp. Fennel seed, divided.

- One tsp. Dried thyme, divided.

- Two lbs. Lean ground beef, divided.

- Two tsps. Salt, divided.

- One tbsp. Olive oil

- One tsp. Black pepper.

- One tsp. Dry basil, divided.

- 2/3 lb. Pepperoni chopped into small pieces.

- Two tbsps. Dry parsley, divided.

- Two eggs.

- 32 ounces ricotta cheese

- Half tsp. ground nutmeg

- 8 -16 ounces mozzarella cheese, grated.

Instructions

1. Heat the oven to 350 degrees.

2. Heat the olive oil in a large pan at moderate temperature. Put garlic, onion, Italian sausage, and half of the ground meat. Cook for approximately 10 minutes.

3. If required, remove the meat mixture. Put 1/2 teaspoon basil, thyme, oregano, fennel seed, salt, black pepper and 1tbsp of brown sugar, one

tablespoon parsley, tomato sauce. Mix, carefully wrap and allow to boil for 1 hour on low flame.

4. Start preparing the ricotta cheese mixture, lasagna noodles and meatballs while the sauce is cooking. Then, in a wide bowl, break one egg. Add the 1/2 cup of Parmesan, oatmeal and the remaining ground meat, basil, fennel, black pepper, thyme, oregano, and salt according to your taste. Merge properly.

5. Shape the meat into balls that have a size of around 1 inch. Please put it on a sprayed pan and bake for 20 minutes, rotating half the way through the cooking time over the meatballs. In the bowl, put the ricotta cheese in it. Add the remaining nutmeg, egg, and the remaining parsley. Merge and set it aside.

6. Then, boil the lasagna noodles for at least 15 minutes in a big pan full of very hot water.

7. The lasagna is placed in a deep 9x3-inch pan till the sauce is cooked. On the base of the pan, pour 2 cups of the sauce. Just lay down six noodles. Layer half of the ricotta on the noodles and top with 1/3 of the parmesan and mozzarella. Place half the pepperoni on top of that.

8. Similarly, make another layer, beginning with 2 cups of sauce. Lay down the remaining portion of the lasagna noodles on top afterward.

9. Blend the rest of the sauce into the cooked meatballs and scatter on top of the lasagna. Cover with a cheese layer.

10. Wrap in foil and bake for 25 minutes at 350F. Let us remove the foil and bake for 25 minutes. Take it out and cool it for 15 minutes before served.

Introduction:

You have got the set of important knives, toaster oven, coffee machine, and quick pot along with the cutter you want to good care of. There may be a variety of things inside your kitchen, but maybe you wish to make more space for an air fryer. It's easy to crowd and load with the new cooking equipment even though you've a lot of them. However, an air fryer is something you will want to make space for.

The air fryer is identical to the oven in the way that it roasts and bakes, but the distinction is that elements of hating are placed over the top& are supported by a big, strong fan, producing food that is extremely crispy and, most importantly with little oil in comparison to the counterparts which are deeply fried. Usually, air fryers heat up pretty fast and, because of the centralized heat source & the fan size and placement, they prepare meals quickly & uniformly. The cleanup is another huge component of the air frying. Many baskets & racks for air fryers are dishwasher protected. We recommend a decent dish brush for those who are not dishwasher secure. It will go through all the crannies and nooks that facilitate the movement of air without making you crazy.

We have seen many rave reviews of this new trend, air frying. Since air frying, they argue, calls for fast and nutritious foods. But is the hype worth it? How do the air fryers work? Does it really fry food?

How do air fryers work?

First, let's consider how air fryer really works before we go to which type of air fryer is decent or any simple recipes. Just think of it; cooking stuff without oil is such a miracle. Then, how could this even be possible? Let's try to find out how to pick the best air fryer for your use now when you understand how the air fryer works.

How to pick the best air fryer

It is common to get lost when purchasing gadgets & electrical equipment, given that there're a wide range of choices available on the market. So, before investing in one, it is really ideal to have in mind the specifications and budget.

Before purchasing the air fryer, you can see the things you should consider:

Capacity/size: Air fryers are of various sizes, from one liter to sixteen liters. A three-liter capacity is fine enough for bachelors. Choose an air fryer that has a range of 4–6 liters for a family having two children. There is a restricted size of the basket which is used to put the food. You will have to prepare the meals in batches if you probably wind up using a tiny air fryer.

Timer: Standard air fryers arrive with a range timer of 30 minutes. For house cooking, it is satisfactory. Thought, if you are trying complex recipes which take a longer cooking time, pick the air fryer with a 1-hour timer.

Temperature: The optimum temperature for most common air fryers is 200 degrees C (400 f). You can quickly prepare meat dishes such as fried chicken, tandoori, kebabs etc.

The design, durability, brand value and controls are other considerations you might consider.

Now that you know which air fryer is best for you let's see the advantages of having an air fryer at your place.

What are the benefits of air fryers?

The benefits of air fryers are as follows:

Cooking with lower fat & will promote weight loss

Air fryers work with no oils and contain up to 80 percent lower fat than most fryers relative to a traditional deep fryer. Shifting to an air fryer may encourage loss of weight by decreasing fat & caloric intake for anyone who consumes fried food regularly and also has a problem with leaving the fast foods.

Faster time for cooking

Air frying is easier comparing with other cooking techniques, such as grilling or baking. Few air fryers need a preheat of 60 seconds, but others do not need a preheat any longer than a grill or an oven. So if there is a greater capacity or multiple compartments for the air fryer basket, you may make various dishes in one go.

Quick to clean

It's extremely easy to clean an air fryer. And after each use, air frying usually does not create enough of a mess except you cook fatty food such as steak or chicken wings. Take the air fryer out and clean it with soap & water in order to disinfect the air fryer.

Safer to be used

The air fryer is having no drawbacks, unlike hot plates or deep frying. Air fryers get hot, but splashing or spilling is not a risk.

Minimum use of electricity and environment friendly

Air fryers consume far less electricity than various electric ovens, saving your money & reducing carbon output.

Flexibility

Some of the air fryers are multi-functional. It's possible to heat, roast, steam, broil, fry or grill food.

Less waste and mess

Pan-fries or deep fryer strategies leave one with excess cooking oil, which is difficult to rid of and usually unsustainable. You can cook fully oil-less food with an air fryer. All the pieces have a coating of nonstick, dishwasher safe and nonstick coating.

Cooking without the use of hands

The air fryer includes a timer, & when it is full, it'll stop by itself so that you may feel secure while multitasking.

Feasible to use

It is very much convenient; you can use an air fryer whenever you want to. Few air fryers involve preheating, which is less than 5 minutes; with the air fryer, one may begin cooking immediately.

Reducing the possibility of the development of toxic acrylamide

Compared to making food in oil, air frying will decrease the potential of producing acrylamides. Acrylamide is a compound that, under elevated temperature cooking, appears in certain food and may have health impacts.

Chapter 1: Air fryer breakfast recipes

133.   1. Air fryer breakfast frittata

Cook time: 20 minutes

Servings: 2 people

Difficulty: Easy

Ingredients:

- 1 pinch of cayenne pepper (not necessary)

- 1 chopped green onion

- Cooking spray

- 2 tbsp. diced red bell pepper

- ¼ pound fully cooked and crumbled breakfast sausages

- 4 lightly beaten eggs

- ½ cup shredded cheddar-Monterey jack cheese blend

Instructions:

1. Combine eggs, bell pepper, cheddar Monterey Jack cheese, sausages, cayenne and onion inside a bowl & blend to combine.

2. The air fryer should be preheated to 360 ° f (180° c). Spray a 6 by 2-inch non-stick cake pan along with a spray used in cooking.

3. Place the mixture of egg in the ready-made cake tray.

4. Cook for 18 - 20 minutes in your air fryer before the frittata is ready.

Cook time: 28 minutes

Serving: 8 people

Difficulty: Easy

Ingredients:

- 3/4 cup flour for all purposes

- 1/4 tbsp. salt

- 1 egg

- 2 mashed bananas overripe

- 1/4 cup sour cream

- 1/2 cup sugar

- 1/4 tbsp. baking soda

- 7-inch bundt pan

- 1/4 cup vegetable oil

- 1/2 tbsp. vanilla

Instructions:

1. In one tub, combine the dry ingredients and the wet ones in another. Mix the two slowly till flour is fully integrated, don't over mix.

2. With an anti-stick spray, spray and on a 7-inch bundt pan & then pour in the bowl.

3. Put it inside the air fryer basket & close. Placed it for 28 mins to 310 degrees

4. Remove when completed & permit to rest in the pan for about 5 mins.

5. When completed, detach and allow 5 minutes to sit in the pan. Then flip on a plate gently. Sprinkle melted icing on top, serve after slicing.

Cook time: 8 minutes

Serving: 2 people

Difficulty: Easy

Ingredients:

- 1/4 cup shredded cheese

- 2 eggs

- Pinch of salt

- 1 teaspoon of McCormick morning breakfast seasoning – garden herb

- Fresh meat & veggies, diced

- 1/4 cup milk

Instructions:

1. In a tiny tub, mix the milk and eggs till all of them are well mixed.

2. Add a little salt in the mixture of an egg.

3. Then, in the mixture of egg, add the veggies.

4. Pour the mixture of egg in a greased pan of 6 by 3 inches.

5. Place your pan inside the air fryer container.

6. Cook for about 8 to 10 mins and at 350 f.

7. While you are cooking, slather the breakfast seasoning over the eggs & slather the cheese on the top.

8. With a thin spoon, loose the omelet from the pan and pass it to a tray.

9. Loosen the omelet from the sides of the pan with a thin spatula and pass it to a tray.

10. Its options to garnish it with additional green onions.

4. Air-fried breakfast bombs

Cook time: 20 mins

Serving: 2

Difficulty: easy

Ingredients:

• Cooking spray

• 1 tbsp. fresh chives chopped

• 3 lightly beaten, large eggs

• 4 ounces whole-wheat pizza dough freshly prepared

• 3 bacon slices center-cut

• 1 ounce 1/3-less-fat softened cream cheese

Instructions:

1. Cook the bacon in a standard size skillet for around 10 minutes, medium to very crisp. Take the bacon out of the pan; scatter. Add the eggs to the bacon drippings inside the pan; then cook, stirring constantly, around 1 minute, until almost firm and yet loose. Place the eggs in a bowl; add the cream cheese, the chives, and the crumbled bacon.

2. Divide the dough into four identical sections. Roll each bit into a five-inch circle on a thinly floured surface. Place a quarter of the egg mixture in the middle of each circle of dough. Clean the underside of the dough with the help of water; wrap the dough all around the mixture of an egg to form a purse and pinch the dough.

3. Put dough purses inside the air fryer basket in one layer; coat really well with the help of cooking spray. Cook for 5 to 6 minutes at 350 degrees f till it turns to a golden brown; check after 4 mins.

5. Air fryer French toast

Cook time: 15 mins

Serving: 2 people

Difficulty: easy

Ingredients:

- 4 beaten eggs

- 4 slices of bread

- Cooking spray (non-stick)

Instructions:

1. Put the eggs inside a container or a bowl which is sufficient and big, so the pieces of bread will fit inside.

2. With a fork, mix the eggs and after that, place each bread slice over the mixture of an egg.

3. Turn the bread for one time so that every side is filled with a mixture of an egg.

4. After that, fold a big sheet of aluminum foil; this will keep the bread together. Switch the foil's side; this will ensure that the mixture of an egg may not get dry. Now put the foil basket in the air fryer basket. Make sure to allow space around the edges; this will let the circulation of hot air.

5. With the help of cooking spray, spray the surface of the foil basket and then put the bread over it. On top, you may add the excess mixture of an egg.

6. For 5 mins, place the time to 365 degrees f.

7. Turn the bread & cook it again for about 3 to 5 mins, until it's golden brown over the top of the French toast & the egg isn't runny.

8. Serve it hot, with toppings of your choice.

Cook time: 15 mins

Servings: 2

Difficulty: easy

Ingredients:

- 1/2 tbsp. kosher salt

- 1/2 tbsp. garlic powder

- Breakfast potato seasoning

- 1/2 tbsp. smoked paprika

- 1 tbsp. oil

- 5 potatoes medium-sized. Peeled & cut to one-inch cubes (Yukon gold works best)

- 1/4 tbsp. black ground pepper

Instructions:

1. At 400 degrees f, preheat the air fryer for around 2 to 3 minutes. Doing this will provide you the potatoes that are crispiest.

2. Besides that, brush your potatoes with oil and breakfast potato seasoning till it is fully coated.

3. Using a spray that's non-stick, spray on the air fryer. Add potatoes & cook for about 15 mins, shaking and stopping the basket for 2 to 3 times so that you can have better cooking.

4. Place it on a plate & serve it immediately.

7. Air fryer breakfast pockets

Cook time: 15 mins

Serving: 5 people

Difficulty: easy

Ingredients:

- 2-gallon zip lock bags

- Salt & pepper to taste

- 1/3 + 1/4 cup of whole milk

- 1 whole egg for egg wash

- Cooking spray

- 1-2 ounces of Velveeta cheese

- Parchment paper

- 1 lb. of ground pork

- 2 packages of Pillsbury pie crust

- 2 crusts to a package

- 4 whole eggs

Instructions:

1. Let the pie crusts out of the freezer.

2. Brown the pig and rinse it.

3. In a tiny pot, heat 1/4 cup of cheese and milk until it is melted.

4. Whisk four eggs, season with pepper and salt & add the rest of the milk.

5. Fumble the eggs in the pan until they are nearly fully cooked.

6. Mix the eggs, cheese and meat together.

7. Roll out the pie crust & cut it into a circle of about 3 to 4 inches (cereal bowl size).

8. Whisk 1 egg for making an egg wash.

9. Put around 2 tbsp. of the blend in the center of every circle.

10. Now, eggs wash the sides of the circle.

11. Create a moon shape by folding the circle.

12. With the help of a fork, folded edges must be crimped

13. Place the pockets inside parchment paper & put it inside a ziplock plastic bag overnight.

14. Preheat the air fryer for 360 degrees until it is ready to serve.

15. With a cooking spray, each pocket side must be sprayed.

16. Put pockets inside the preheated air fryer for around 15 mins or till they are golden brown.

17. Take it out from the air fryer & make sure it's cool before you serve it.

140.   8. Air fryer sausage breakfast casserole

Cook time: 20 mins

Serving: 6 people

Difficulty: easy

Ingredients:

- 1 diced red bell pepper

- 1 lb. ground breakfast sausage

- 4 eggs

- 1 diced green bell pepper

- 1/4 cup diced sweet onion

- 1 diced yellow bell pepper

- 1 lb. hash browns

Instructions:

1. Foil line your air fryer's basket.

2. At the bottom, put some hash browns.

3. Cover it with the raw sausage.

4. Place the onions & peppers uniformly on top.

5. Cook for 10 mins at 355 degrees.

6. Open your air fryer & blend the casserole a little if necessary.

7. Break every egg inside the bowl and spill it directly over the casserole.

8. Cook for the next 10 minutes for 355 degrees.

9. Serve with pepper and salt for taste.

Cook time: 15 mins

Servings: 6 people

Difficulty: easy

Ingredients:

- Black pepper, to taste

- 6 large eggs

- Olive oil spray

- 2 tbsp. chopped green onions

- 1 tablespoon water

- 1/4 teaspoon kosher salt

- 2 tablespoons diced red bell pepper

- 1/2 pound turkey or chicken sausage

- 12 egg roll wrappers

- The salsa that is optional for dipping

Instructions:

1. Combine the water, salt and black pepper with the eggs.

2. Cook sausage in a non-stick skillet of medium size, make sure to let it cook in medium heat till there's no pink color left for 4 minutes, splitting into crumbles, then drain.

3. Stir in peppers and scallions & cook it for 2 minutes. Put it on a plate.

4. Over moderate flame, heat your skillet & spray it with oil.

5. Pour the egg mixture & cook stirring till the eggs are cooked and fluffy. Mix the sausage mixture.

6. Put one wrapped egg roll on a dry, clean work surface having corners aligned like it's a diamond.

7. Include an egg mixture of 1/4 cup on the lower third of your wrapper.

8. Gently raise the lower point closest to you & tie it around your filling.

9. Fold the right & left corners towards the middle & continue rolling into the compact cylinder.

10. Do this again with the leftover wrappers and fillings.

11. Spray oil on every side of your egg roll & rub it with hands to cover them evenly.

12. The air fryer must be preheated to 370 degrees f.

13. Cook the egg rolls for about 10 minutes in batches till it's crispy and golden brown.

14. Serve instantly with salsa, if required.

Cook time: 45 mins

Servings: 6 people

Difficulty: medium

Ingredients:

- 1 tbsp. extra virgin olive oil

- Salt and pepper

- 4 bacon rashers

- 1 tbsp. oregano

- 1 tbsp. garlic powder

- 2 bread rolls stale

- 1 tbsp. parsley

- 320 grams grated cheese

- 4 sweet potatoes of medium size

- 3 spring onions

- 8 pork sausages of medium size

- 11 large eggs

- 1 bell pepper

Instructions:

1. Dice and peel the sweet potato in cubes. Mix the garlic, salt, oregano and pepper in a bowl with olive oil of extra virgin.

2. In an air fryer, put your sweet potatoes. Dice the mixed peppers, cut the sausages in quarters & dice the bacon.

3. Add the peppers, bacon and sausages over the sweet potatoes. Air fry it at 160c or 320 f for 15 mins.

4. Cube and slice the bread when your air fryer is heating & pound your eggs in a blending jug with the eggs, including some extra parsley along with pepper and salt. Dice the spring onion.

5. Check the potatoes when you hear a beep from the air fryer. A fork is needed to check on the potatoes. If you are unable to, then cook for a further 2 to 3 minutes. Mix the basket of the air fryer, include the spring onions & then cook it for an additional five minutes with the same temperature and cooking time.

6. Using the projected baking pans, place the components of your air fryer on 2 of them. Mix it while adding bread and cheese. Add your mixture of egg on them & they are primed for the actual air fry.

7. Put the baking pan inside your air fryer & cook for 25 minutes for 160 c or 320 f. If you planned to cook 2, cook 1 first and then the other one. Place a cocktail stick into the middle & then it's done if it comes out clear and clean.

Cook time: 10 mins

Serving: 2 people

Difficulty: easy

Ingredients:

- 1 pound breakfast sausage

- Air fryer breakfast sausage ingredients

Instructions:

1. Insert your sausage links in the basket of an air fryer.

2. Cook your sausages or the sausage links for around 8 to 10 minutes at 360°.

144.   12. Wake up air fryer avocado boats

Cook time: 5 mins

Servings: 2

Difficulty: easy

Ingredients:

- 1/2 teaspoon salt

- 2 plum tomatoes, seeded & diced

- 1/4 teaspoon black pepper

- 1 tablespoon finely diced jalapeno (optional)

- 4 eggs (medium or large recommended)

- 1/4 cup diced red onion

- 2 avocados, halved & pitted

- 1 tablespoon lime juice

- 2 tablespoons chopped fresh cilantro

Instructions:

1. Squeeze the avocado fruit out from the skin with a spoon, leaving the shell preserved. Dice the avocado and put it in a bowl of medium-sized. Combine it with onion, jalapeno (if there is a need), tomato, pepper and cilantro. Refrigerate and cover the mixture of avocado until ready for usage.

2. Preheat the air-fryer for 350° f

3. Place the avocado shells on a ring made up of failing to make sure they don't rock when cooking. Just roll 2 three-inch-wide strips of aluminum foil into rope shapes to create them, and turn each one into a three-inch circle. In an air fryer basket, put every avocado shell over a foil frame. Break an egg in every avocado shell & air fry for 5 - 7 minutes or when needed.

4. Take it out from the basket; fill including avocado salsa & serve.

145.   12. Air fryer cinnamon rolls

Cook time: 15 mins

Serving: 2 people

Difficulty: easy

Ingredients:

- 1 spray must non-stick cooking spray

- 1 can cinnamon rolls we used Pillsbury

Instructions:

1. put your cinnamon rolls inside your air fryer's basket, with the help of the rounds of 2. Parchment paper or by the cooking spray that is non-stick.

2. Cook at around 340 degrees f, 171 degrees for about 12 to 15 minutes, for one time.

3. Drizzle it with icing, place it on a plate and then serve.

146.   13. Air-fryer all-American breakfast dumplings

Cook: 10 minutes

Servings: 1 person

Difficulty: easy

Ingredients:

- Dash salt

- 1/2 cup (about four large) egg whites or liquid egg fat-free substitute

- 1 tbsp. Pre-cooked real crumbled bacon

- 1 wedge the laughing cow light creamy Swiss cheese (or 1 tbsp. reduced-fat cream cheese)

- 8 wonton wrappers or gyoza

Instructions:

1. By using a non-stick spray, spray your microwave-safe bowl or mug. Include egg whites or any substitute, salt and cheese wedge. Microwave it for around 1.5 minutes, mixing in between until cheese gets well mixed and melted and the egg is set.

2. Mix the bacon in. Let it cool completely for about 5 minutes.

3. Cover a wrapper of gyoza with the mixture of an egg (1 tablespoon). Moist the corners with water & fold it in half, having the filling. Tightly push the corners to seal. Repeat this step to make seven more dumplings. Make sure to use a non-stick spray for spraying.

4. Insert the dumplings inside your air fryer in one single layer. (Save the leftover for another round if they all can't fit). Adjust the temperature to 375 or the closest degree. Cook it for around 5 mins or till it's crispy and golden brown.

Chapter 2: Air fryer seafood recipe

147.   1. Air fryer 'shrimp boil'

Cook time: 15 mins

Servings: 2 people

Difficulty: easy

Ingredients:

- 2 tbsp. vegetable oil

- 1 lb. easy-peel defrosted shrimp

- 3 small red potatoes cut 1/2 inch rounds

- 1 tbsp. old bay seasoning

- 2 ears of corn cut into thirds

- 14 oz. smoked sausage, cut into three-inch pieces

Instructions:

1. Mix all the items altogether inside a huge tub & drizzle it with old bay seasoning, peppers, oil and salt. Switch to the air fryer basket attachment & place the basket over the pot.

2. Put inside your air fryer & adjust the setting of fish; make sure to flip after seven minutes.

3. Cautiously remove & then serve.

Cook time: 10 mins

Serving: 6 people

Difficulty: easy

Ingredients:

- Tartar sauce for serving

- ½ tbsp. garlic powder

- 1 pound cod fillet cut into strips

- Black pepper

- 2 cups panko breadcrumbs

- ½ cup all-purpose flour

- ¼ tbsp. salt

- Large egg beaten

- Lemon wedges for serving

- 2 teaspoons paprika

Instructions:

1. In a tiny tub, combine the flour, adding salt, paprika and garlic powder. Put your beaten egg in one bowl & your panko breadcrumbs in another bowl.

2. Wipe your fish dry with a towel. Dredge your fish with the mixture of flour, now the egg & gradually your panko breadcrumbs, pushing down gently till your crumbs stick. Spray both ends with oil.

3. Fry at 400 degrees f. Now turn halfway for around 10 to 12 mins until it's lightly brown and crispy.

4. Open your basket & search for preferred crispiness with the help of a fork to know if it easily flakes off. You may hold fish for an extra 1 to 2 mins as required.

5. Serve instantly with tartar sauce and fries, if required.

149.   3. Air-fryer scallops

Cook time: 20 mins

Servings: 2 people

Difficulty: easy

Ingredients:

- ¼ cup extra-virgin olive oil

- ½ tbsp. garlic finely chopped

- Cooking spray

- ½ teaspoons finely chopped garlic

- 8 large (1-oz.) Sea scallops, cleaned & patted very dry

- 1 tbsp. finely grated lemon zest

- ⅛ tbsp. salt

- 2 tbsps. Very finely chopped flat-leaf parsley

- 2 tbsp. capers, very finely chopped

- ¼ tbsp. ground pepper

Instructions:

1. Sprinkle the scallops with salt and pepper. Cover the air fryer basket by the cooking spray. Put your scallops inside the basket & cover them by the cooking spray. Put your basket inside the air fryer. Cook your scallops at a degree of 400 f till they attain the temperature of about 120 degrees f, which is an international temperature for 6 mins.

2. Mix capers, oil, garlic, lemon zest and parsley inside a tiny tub. Sprinkle over your scallops.

150.   4. Air fryer tilapia

Cook time: 6 mins

Servings: 4 people

Difficulty: easy

Ingredients:

- 1/2 tbsp. paprika

- 1 tbsp. salt

- 2 eggs

- 4 fillets of tilapia

- 1 tbsp. garlic powder

- 1/2 teaspoon black pepper

- 1/2 cup flour

- 2 tbsp. lemon zest

- 1 tbsp. garlic powder

- 4 ounces parmesan cheese, grated

Instructions:

1. Cover your tilapia fillets:

Arrange three deep dishes. Out of these, put flour in one. Blend egg in second and make sure that the eggs are whisked in the last dish mix lemon zest, cheese, pepper, paprika and salt. Ensure that the tilapia fillets are dry, and after that dip, every fillet inside the flour & covers every side. Dip into your egg wash & pass them for coating every side of the fillet to your cheese mixture.

2. Cook your tilapia:

Put a tiny sheet of parchment paper in your bask of air fryer and put 1 - 2 fillets inside the baskets. Cook at 400°f for around 4 - 5 minutes till the crust seems golden brown, and the cheese completely melts.

Cook time: 7 mins

Serving: 2 people

Difficulty: easy

Ingredients:

- 1/2 tbsp. salt

- 2 tbsp. olive oil

- 1/4 teaspoon ground black pepper

- 2 salmon fillets (about 1 1/2-inches thick)

- 1/2 teaspoon ginger powder

- 2 teaspoons smoked paprika

- 1 teaspoon onion powder

- 1/4 teaspoon red pepper flakes

- 1 tbsp. garlic powder

- 1 tablespoon brown sugar (optional)

Instructions:

1. Take the fish out of the refrigerator, check if there are any bones, & let it rest for 1 hour on the table.

2. Combine all the ingredients in a tub.

3. Apply olive oil in every fillet & then the dry rub solution.

4. Put the fillets in the Air Fryer basket.

5. set the air fryer for 7 minutes at the degree of 390 if your fillets have a thickness of 1-1/2-inches.

6. As soon as the timer stops, test fillets with a fork's help to ensure that they are ready to the perfect density. If you see that there is any need, then you cook it for a further few minutes. Your cooking time may vary with the temperature & size of the fish. It is best to set your air fryer for a minimum time, and then you may increase the time if there is a need. This will prevent the fish from being overcooked.

6. Blackened fish tacos in the air fryer

Cook time: 9 mins

Serving: 4 people

Difficulty: easy

Ingredients:

- 1 lb. Mahi mahi fillets (can use cod, catfish, tilapia or salmon)

- Cajun spices blend (or use 2-2.5 tbsp. store-bought Cajun spice blend)

- ¾ teaspoon salt

- 1 tbsp. paprika (regular, not smoked)

- 1 teaspoon oregano

- ½-¾ teaspoon cayenne (reduces or skips to preference)

- ½ teaspoon garlic powder

- ½ teaspoon onion powder

- ½ teaspoon black pepper

- 1 teaspoon brown sugar (skip for low-carb)

Additional ingredients for tacos:

- Mango salsa

- Shredded cabbage (optional)

- 8 corn tortillas

Instructions:

1. Get the fish ready

2. Mix cayenne, onion powder, brown sugar, salt, oregano, garlic powder, paprika and black pepper in a deep mixing tub.

3. Make sure to get the fish dry by using paper towels. Drizzle or brush the fish with a little amount of any cooking oil or olive oil. This allows the spices to stick to the fish.

4. Sprinkle your spice mix graciously on a single edge of your fish fillets. Rub the fish softly, so the ingredients stay on the fish.

5. Flip and brush the fish with oil on the other side & sprinkle with the leftover spices. Press the ingredients inside the fish softly.

6. Turn the air fryer on. Inside the basket put your fish fillets. Do not overlap the pan or overfill it. Close your basket.

7. Air fry the fish

8. Set your air fryer for 9 mins at 360°f. If you are using fillets which are thicker than an inch, then you must increase the cooking time to ten minutes. When the air fryer timer stops, with the help of a fish spatula or long tongs, remove your fish fillets.

9. Assembling the tacos

10. Heat the corn tortillas according to your preference. Conversely, roll them inside the towel made up of wet paper & heat them in the microwave for around 20 to 30 seconds.

11. Stack 2 small fillets or insert your fish fillet. Add a few tablespoons of your favorite mango salsa or condiment & cherish the scorched fish tacos.

12. Alternatively, one can include a few cabbages shredded inside the tacos & now add fish fillets on the top.

153.   7. Air fryer cod

Cook time: 16 mins

Servings: 2 people

Difficulty: easy

Ingredients:

- 2 teaspoon of light oil for spraying

- 1 cup of plantain flour

- 0.25 teaspoon of salt

- 12 pieces of cod about 1 ½ pound

- 1 teaspoon of garlic powder

- 0.5 cup gluten-free flour blend

- 2 teaspoon of smoked paprika

- 4 teaspoons of Cajun seasoning or old bay

- Pepper to taste

Instructions:

1. Spray some oil on your air fryer basket & heat it up to 360° f.

2. Combine the ingredients in a tub & whisk them to blend. From your package, take the cod out and, with the help of a paper towel, pat dry.

3. Dunk every fish piece in the mixture of flour spice and flip it over & push down so that your fish can be coated.

4. Get the fish inside the basket of your air fryer. Ensure that there is room around every fish piece so that the air can flow round the fish.

5. Cook for around 8 minutes & open your air fryer so that you can flip your fish. Now cook another end for around 8 mins.

6. Now cherish the hot serving with lemon.

154.   8. Air fryer miso-glazed Chilean sea bass

Cook time: 20 mins

Serving: 2 people

Difficulty: easy

Ingredients:

- 1/2 teaspoon ginger paste

- Fresh cracked pepper

- 1 tbsp. unsalted butter

- Olive oil for cooking

- 1 tbsp. rice wine vinegar

- 2 tbsp. miring

- 1/4 cup white miso paste

- 2 6 ounce Chilean sea bass fillets

- 4 tbsp. Maple syrup, honey works too.

Instructions:

1. Heat your air fryer to 375 degrees f. Apply olive oil onto every fish fillet and complete it with fresh pepper. Sprat olive oil on the pan of the air fryer and put the skin of the fish. Cook for about 12 to 15 minutes till you see the upper part change into golden brown color & the inner temperature now reached 135-degree f.

2. When the fish is getting cooked, you must have the butter melted inside a tiny saucepan in medium heat. When you notice that the butter melts, add maple syrup, ginger paste, miso paste, miring and rice wine vinegar, mix all of them till they are completely combined, boil them in a light flame and take the pan out instantly from the heat.

3. When your fish is completely done, brush the glaze and fish sides with the help of silicone pastry. Put it back inside your air fryer for around 1 to 2 extra minutes at 375 degrees f, till the glaze is caramelized. Complete it with green onion (sliced) & sesame seeds.

Instructions for oven

1. Heat the oven around 425 degrees f and put your baking sheet and foil sprayed with light olive oil. Bake it for about 20 to 25 minutes; this depends on how thick the fish is. The inner temperature must be around 130 degrees f when your fish is completely cooked.

2. Take out your fish, placed it in the oven & heat the broiler on a high flame. Now the fish must be brushed with miso glaze from the sides and the top & then put the

fish inside the oven in the above rack. If the rack is very much near with your broiler, then place it a bit down, you might not want the fish to touch the broiler. Cook your fish for around 1 to 2 minutes above the broiler till you see it's getting caramelize. Make sure to keep a check on it as it happens very quickly. Complete it with the help of green onions (sliced) and sesame seeds.

Cook time: 35 mins

Serving: 6 people

Difficulty: Medium

Ingredients:

- ¼ teaspoon salt

- ¼ cup thinly sliced red onion

- 1 tbsp. water

- 2 tbsp. sour cream

- Sliced avocado, thinly sliced radishes, chopped fresh cilantro leaves and lime wedges

- 1 teaspoon lime juice

- ½ lb. skinless white fish fillets (such as halibut or mahi-mahi), cut into 1-inch strips

- 1 tbsp. mayonnaise

- 1 egg

- 1 package (12 bowls) old el Paso mini flour tortilla taco bowls, heated as directed on package

- 1 clove garlic, finely chopped

- ½ cup Progresso plain panko crispy bread crumbs

- 1 ½ cups shredded green cabbage

- 2 tbsp. old el Paso original taco seasoning mix (from 1-oz package)

Instructions:

1. Combine the sour cream, garlic, salt, mayonnaise and lime juice together in a medium pot. Add red onion and cabbage; flip to coat. Refrigerate and cover the mixture of cabbage until fit for serving.

2. Cut an 8-inch circle of parchment paper for frying. Place the basket at the bottom of the air fryer.

3. Place the taco-seasoning mix in a deep bowl. Beat the egg & water in another small bowl. Place the bread crumbs in another shallow dish. Coat the fish with your taco seasoning mix; dip inside the beaten egg, then cover with the mixture of bread crumbs, pressing to hold to it.

156. 10. Air fryer southern fried catfish

Cook time: 13 mins

Servings: 4 people

Difficulty: easy

Ingredients:

- 1 lemon

- 1/4 teaspoon cayenne pepper

- Cornmeal seasoning mix

- 1/4 teaspoon granulated onion powder

- 1/2 cup cornmeal

- 1/2 teaspoon kosher salt

- 1/4 teaspoon chili powder

- 2 pounds catfish fillets

- 1/4 teaspoon garlic powder

- 1 cup milk

- 1/4 cup all-purpose flour

- 1/4 teaspoon freshly ground black pepper

- 2 tbsp. dried parsley flakes

- 1/2 cup yellow mustard

Instructions:

1. Add milk and put the catfish in a flat dish.

2. Slice the lemon in two & squeeze around two tbsp. of juice added into milk so that the buttermilk can be made.

3. Place the dish in the refrigerator & leave it for 15 minutes to soak the fillets.

4. Combine the cornmeal-seasoning mixture in a small bowl.

5. Take the fillets out from the buttermilk & pat them dry with the help of paper towels.

6. Spread the mustard evenly on both sides of the fillets.

7. Dip every fillet into a mixture of cornmeal & coat well to create a dense coating.

8. Place the fillets in the greased basket of the air fryer. Spray gently with olive oil.

9. Cook for around 10 minutes at 390 to 400 degrees. Turn over the fillets & spray them with oil & cook for another 3 to 5 mins.

Cook time: 8 mins

Serving: 2 people

Difficulty: easy

Ingredients:

- 1 tbsp. fresh lemon juice

- 2 till 6 oz. Lobster tails, thawed

- Fresh chopped parsley for garnish (optional)

- 4 tbsp. melted salted butter

Instructions:

1. Make lemon butter combining lemon and melted butter. Mix properly & set aside.

2. Wash lobster tails & absorb the water with a paper towel. Butter your lobster tails by breaking the shell, take out the meat & place it over the shell.

3. Preheat the air fryer for around 5 minutes to 380 degrees. Place the ready lobster tails inside the basket of air fryer, drizzle with single tbsp. melted lemon butter on the meat of lobster. Cover the basket of the air fryer and cook for around 8 minutes at 380 degrees f, or when the lobster meat is not translucent. Open the air fryer halfway into the baking time, and then drizzle with extra lemon butter. Continue to bake until finished.

4. Remove the lobster tails carefully, garnish with crushed parsley if you want to, & plate. For dipping, serve with additional lemon butter.

Cook time: 20 mins

Servings: 2 people

Difficulty: easy

Ingredients:

For the crab cakes:

- 1. Avocado oil spray

- 16-ounce lump crab meat

- 1 egg, lightly beaten

- 2 tbsp. finely chopped red or orange pepper

- 1 tbsp. Dijon mustard

- 2 tbsp. finely chopped green onion

- 1/4 teaspoon ground pepper

- 1/4 cup panko breadcrumbs

- 2 tbsp. olive oil mayonnaise

For the aioli:

- 1/4 teaspoon cayenne pepper

- 1/4 cup olive oil mayonnaise

- 1 teaspoon white wine vinegar

- 1 teaspoon minced shallots

- 1 teaspoon Dijon mustard

For the vinaigrette:

- 2 tbsp. extra virgin olive oil

- 1 tbsp. white wine vinegar

- 4 tbsp. fresh lemon juice, about 1 ½ lemon

- 1 teaspoon honey

- 1 teaspoon lemon zest

To serve:

- Balsamic glaze, to taste

- 2 cups of baby arugula

Instructions:

1. Make your crab cake. Mix red pepper, mayonnaise, ground pepper, crab meat, onion, panko and Dijon in a huge bowl. Make sure to mix the ingredients well. Then add eggs & mix the mixture again till it's mixed well. Take around 1/4 cup of the mixture of crab into cakes which are around 1 inch thick. Spray with avocado oil gently.

2. Cook your crab cakes. Organize crab cakes in one layer in the air fryer. It depends on the air fryer how many batches will be required to cook them. Cook for 10 minutes at 375 degrees f. Take it out from your air fryer & keep it warm. Do this again if required.

3. Make aioli. Combine shallots, Dijon, vinegar, cayenne pepper and mayo. Put aside for serving until ready.

4. Make the vinaigrette. Combine honey, white vinegar, and lemon zest and lemon juice in a ting jar. Include olive oil & mix it well until mixed together.

5. Now serve. Split your arugula into 2 plates. Garnish with crab cakes. Drizzle it with vinaigrette & aioli. Include few drizzles of balsamic glaze if desired.

Chapter 3: Air Fryer Meat and Beef recipe

159.   1. Air fryer steak

Cook time: 35 mins

Servings: 2

Difficulty: Medium

Ingredients:

• Freshly ground black pepper

• 1 tsp. freshly chopped chives

• 2 cloves garlic, minced

• 1(2 lb.) Bone-in rib eye

• 4 tbsp. Butter softened

• 1 tsp. Rosemary freshly chopped

• 2 tsp. Parsley freshly chopped

• 1 tsp. Thyme freshly chopped

• Kosher salt

Instructions:

1. In a tiny bowl, mix herbs and butter. Put a small layer of the wrap made up of plastic & roll in a log. Twist the ends altogether to make it refrigerate and tight till it gets hardened for around 20 minutes.

2. Season the steak with pepper and salt on every side.

3. Put the steak in the air-fryer basket & cook it around 400 degrees for 12 - 14 minutes, in medium temperature, depending on the thickness of the steak, tossing half-way through.

4. Cover your steak with the herb butter slice to serve.

160.   2. Air-fryer ground beef wellington

Cook time: 20 mins

Serving: 2 people

Difficulty: easy

Ingredients:

• 1 large egg yolk

• 1 tsp. dried parsley flakes

• 2 tsp. flour for all-purpose

• 1/2 cup fresh mushrooms chopped

• 1 tbsp. butter

• 1/2 pound of ground beef

• 1 lightly beaten, large egg, it's optional

• 1/4 tsp. of pepper, divided

• 1/4 tsp. of salt

• 1 tube (having 4 ounces) crescent rolls refrigerated

• 2 tbsp. onion finely chopped

- 1/2 cup of half & half cream

Instructions:

1. Preheat the fryer to 300 degrees. Heat the butter over a moderate flame in a saucepan. Include mushrooms; stir, and cook for 5-6 minutes, until tender. Add flour & 1/8 of a tsp. of pepper when mixed. Add cream steadily. Boil it; stir and cook until thickened, for about 2 minutes. Take it out from heat & make it aside.

2. Combine 2 tbsp. of mushroom sauce, 1/8 tsp. of the remaining pepper, onion and egg yolk in a tub. Crumble over the mixture of beef and blend properly. Shape it into two loaves. Unroll and divide the crescent dough into two rectangles; push the perforations to close. Put meatloaf over every rectangle. Bring together the sides and press to seal. Brush it with one beaten egg if necessary.

3. Place the wellingtons on the greased tray inside the basket of the air fryer in a single sheet. Cook till see the thermometer placed into the meatloaf measures 160 degrees, 18 to 22 minutes and until you see golden brown color.

Meanwhile, under low pressure, warm the leftover sauce; mix in the parsley. Serve your sauce, adding wellington.

161.   **3. Air-fried burgers**

Cook time: 10 mins

Serving: 4 people

Difficulty: easy

Ingredients:

- 500 g of raw ground beef (1 lb.)

- 1 tsp. of Maggi seasoning sauce

- 1/2 tsp. of ground black pepper

- 1 tsp. parsley (dried)

- Liquid smoke (some drops)

- 1/2 tsp. of salt (salt sub)

- 1 tbsp. of Worcestershire sauce

- 1/2 tsp. of onion powder

- 1/2 tsp. of garlic powder

Instructions:

1. Spray the above tray, and set it aside. You don't have to spray your basket if you are having an air fryer of basket-type. The cooking temperature for basket types will be around 180 c or 350 f.

2. Mix all the spice things together in a little tub, such as the sauce of Worcestershire and dried parsley.

2. In a huge bowl, add it inside the beef.

3. Mix properly, and make sure to overburden the meat as this contributes to hard burgers.

4. Divide the mixture of beef into four, & the patties are to be shape off. Place your indent in the middle with the thumb to keep the patties from scrunching up on the center.

5. Place tray in the air fry; gently spray the surfaces of patties.

6. Cook for around 10 minutes over medium heat (or more than that to see that your food is complete). You don't have to turn your patties.

7. Serve it hot on a pan with your array of side dishes.

162.   4. Air fryer meatloaf

Cook time: 25 mins

Serving: 4 people

Difficulty: easy

Ingredients:

- 1/2 tsp. of Salt

- 1 tsp. of Worcestershire sauce

- 1/2 finely chopped, small onion

- 1 tbsp. of Yellow mustard

- 2 tbsp. of ketchup, divided

- 1 lb. Lean ground beef

- 1/2 tsp. Garlic powder

- 1/4 cup of dry breadcrumbs

- 1 egg, lightly beaten

- 1/4 tsp. Pepper

- 1 tsp. Italian seasoning

Instructions:

1. Put the onion, 1 tbsp. Ketchup, garlic powder, pepper, ground beef, egg, salt, breadcrumbs, Italian seasoning and Worcestershire sauce in a huge bowl.

2. Use hands to blend your spices with the meat equally, be careful you don't over-mix as it would make it difficult to over mix.

3. Shape meat having two inches height of 4 by 6, loaf. Switch your air fryer to a degree of 370 f & Put that loaf inside your air fryer.

4. Cook for fifteen min at a degree of 370 f.

5. In the meantime, mix the leftover 1 tbsp. of ketchup & the mustard in a tiny bowl.

6. Take the meatloaf out of the oven & spread the mixture of mustard over it.

7. Return the meatloaf to your air fryer & begin to bake at a degree of 370 degrees f till the thermometer placed inside the loaf measures 160 degrees f, around 8 to 10 further minutes.

8. Remove the basket from your air fryer when the meatloaf has touched 160 degrees f & then make the loaf stay inside the air fryer basket for around 5 to 10 minutes, after that slice your meatloaf.

Cook time: 16 mins

Serving: 4 people

Difficulty: easy

Ingredients:

- 1 tsp. of onion powder

- 1 pound of ground beef (we are using 85/15)

- 4 pieces burger buns

- 1 tsp. salt

- 1/4 tsp. of black pepper

- 1 tsp. of garlic powder

- 1 tsp. of Worcestershire sauce

Instructions:

1. Method for standard ground beef:

2. Your air fryer must be preheated to 360 °.

3. In a bowl, put the unprocessed ground beef & add the seasonings.

4. To incorporate everything, make the of use your hands (or you can use a fork) & then shape the mixture in a ball shape (still inside the bowl).

5. Score the mixture of ground beef into 4 equal portions by having a + mark to split it.

Scoop out and turn each segment into a patty.

6. Place it in the air fryer, ensuring each patty has plenty of room to cook (make sure not to touch). If required, one can perform this in groups. We've got a bigger (5.8 quart) air fryer, and we did all of ours in a single batch.

7. Cook, turning half-way back, for 16 minutes. (Note: for bigger patties, you may have a need to cook longer.)

Process for Patties (pre-made):

1. In a tiny bowl, mix onion powder, pepper, garlic powder and salt, then stir till well mixed.

2. In a tiny bowl, pour in a few quantities of Worcestershire sauce. You may require A little more than one teaspoon (such as 1.5 tsp.), as some of it will adhere in your pastry brush.

3. Put patties on a tray & spoon or brush on a thin layer of your Worcestershire sauce.

4. Sprinkle with seasoning on every patty, saving 1/2 for another side.

5. With your hand, rub the seasoning to allow it to stick better.

6. Your air fryer should be preheated to 360 ° f.

7. Take out the basket when it's preheated & gently place your patties, seasoned one down, inside the basket.

8. Side 2 of the season, which is facing up the exact way as per above.

9. In an air fryer, put the basket back and cook for around 16 minutes, tossing midway through.

Cook time: 25 mins

Serving: 4 people

Difficulty: Easy

Ingredients:

- Ground black pepper for taste

- 1 tbsp. of olive oil, or as required

- 1 egg, lightly beaten

- 1 tsp. of salt

- 1 pound of lean ground beef

- 1 tbsp. fresh thyme chopped

- 3 tbsp. of dry bread crumbs

- 1 finely chopped, small onion

- 2 thickly sliced mushrooms

Instructions:

1. Preheat your air fryer to a degree of 392 f (200°C).

2. Mix together egg, onion, salt, ground beef, pepper, bread crumbs and thyme in a tub. 3. Thoroughly knead & mix.

4. Transfer the mixture of beef in your baking pan & smooth out the surface. The mushrooms are to be pressed from the top & coated with the olive oil. Put the pan inside the basket of the air fryer & slide it inside your air fryer.

5. Set the timer of the air fryer for around 25 minutes & roast the meatloaf till it is nicely browned.

6. Make sure that the meatloaf stays for a minimum of 10 minutes, and after that, you can slice and serve.

165.   7. Air Fryer Beef Kabobs

Cook time: 8 mins

Serving: 4 people

Difficulty: Easy

Ingredients:

- 1 big onion in red color or onion which you want

- 1.5 pounds of sirloin steak sliced into one-inch chunks

- 1 large bell pepper of your choice

For the marinade:

- 1 tbsp. of lemon juice

- Pinch of Salt & pepper

- 4 tbsp. of olive oil

- 1/2 tsp. of cumin

- 1/2 tsp. of chili powder

- 2 cloves garlic minced

Ingredients:

1. In a huge bowl, mix the beef & ingredients to marinade till fully mixed. Cover & marinate for around 30 minutes or up to 24 hours inside the fridge.

2. Preheat your air fryer to a degree of 400 f until prepared to cook. Thread the onion, pepper and beef onto skewers.

3. Put skewers inside the air fryer, which is already heated and the air fryer for about 8 to 10 minutes, rotating half-way until the outside is crispy and the inside is tender.

166.   8. Air-Fried Beef and Vegetable Skewers

Cook time: 8 mins

Serving: 2

Difficulty: easy

Ingredients:

- 2 tbs. of olive oil

- 2 tsp. of fresh cilantro chopped

- Kosher salt & freshly black pepper ground

- 1 tiny yellow summer squash, sliced into one inch (of 2.5-cm) pieces

- 1/4 tsp. of ground coriander

- Lemon wedges to serve (optional)

- 1/8 tsp. of red pepper flakes

- 1 garlic clove, minced

- 1/2 tsp. of ground cumin

- 1/2 yellow bell pepper, sliced into one inch (that's 2.5-cm) pieces

- 1/2 red bell pepper, sliced into one inch (that's 2.5-cm) pieces

- 1/2 lb. (that's 250 g) boneless sirloin, sliced into one inch (of 2.5-cm) cubes

- 1 tiny zucchini, sliced into one inch (that's 2.5-cm) pieces

- 1/2 red onion, sliced into one inch (that's 2.5-cm) pieces

Ingredients:

1. Preheat your air fryer at 390 degrees f (199-degree c).

2. In a tiny bowl, mix together one tablespoon of cumin, red pepper flakes and coriander. Sprinkle the mixture of spices generously over the meat.

3. In a tub, mix together zucchini, oil, cilantro, bell peppers, summer squash, cilantro, onion and garlic. Season with black pepper and salt to taste.

4. Tightly thread the vegetables and meat onto the four skewers adding two layers rack of air fryer, rotating the bits and equally splitting them. Put the skewers over the rack & carefully set your rack inside the cooking basket. Put the basket inside the air fryer. Cook, without covering it for around 7 - 8 minutes, till the vegetables are crispy and tender & your meat is having a medium-rare.

5. Move your skewers to a tray, and if you want, you can serve them with delicious lemon wedges.

167.   **9. Air fryer taco calzones**

Cook time: 10 mins

Serving: 2 people

Difficulty: easy

Ingredients:

• 1 cup of taco meat

• 1 tube of Pillsbury pizza dough thinly crust

• 1 cup of shredded cheddar

Instructions:

1. Spread out the layer of your pizza dough over a clean table. Slice the dough into four squares with the help of a pizza cutter.

2. By the use of a pizza cutter, cut every square into a big circle. Place the dough pieces aside to create chunks of sugary cinnamon.

3. Cover 1/2 of every dough circle with around 1/4 cup of taco meat & 1/4 cup of shredded cheese.

4. To seal it firmly, fold the remaining over the cheese and meat and push the sides of your dough along with the help of a fork so that it can be tightly sealed. Repeat for all 4 calzones.

5. Each calzone much is gently picked up & spray with olive oil or pan spray. Organize them inside the basket of Air Fryer.

Cook your calzones at a degree of 325 for almost 8 to 10 minutes. Monitor them carefully when it reaches to 8 min mark. This is done so that there is no chance of overcooking.

6. Using salsa & sour cream to serve.

7. For the making of cinnamon sugary chunks, split the dough pieces into pieces having equal sides of around 2 inches long. Put them inside the basket of the air fryer & cook it at a degree of 325 for around 5 minutes. Instantly mix with the one ratio four sugary cinnamon mixtures.

168.   10. Air Fryer Pot Roast

Cook time: 30 mins

Serving: 2 people

Difficulty: Medium

Ingredients:

- 1 tsp. of salt

- 3 tbsp. of brown sugar

- 1/2 cup of orange juice

- 1 tsp. of Worcestershire sauce

- 1/2 tsp. of pepper

- 3–4 pound thawed roast beef chuck roast

- 3 tbsp. of soy sauce

Instructions:

1. Combine brown sugar, Worcestershire sauce, soy sauce and orange juice.

2. Mix till the sugar is completely dissolved.

3. Spillover the roast & marinade for around 8 to 24 hours.

4. Put the roast in the basket of an air fryer.

5. Sprinkle the top with pepper and salt.

6. Air fry it at a degree of 400 f for around 30 minutes, turning it half-way through.

7. Allow it to pause for a period of 3 minutes.

8. Slice and serve into thick cuts.

Chapter 4: midnight snacks

169.   1. Air fryer onion rings

Cook time: 7 mins

Serving: 2 people

Difficulty: easy

Ingredients:

- 2 beaten, large eggs

- Marinara sauce for serving

- 1 ½ tsp. of kosher salt

- ½ tsp. of garlic powder

- 1 medium yellow onion, cut into half in about (1 1/4 cm)

- 1 cup of flour for all-purpose (125 g)

- 1 ½ cups of panko breadcrumbs (172 g)

- 1 tsp. of paprika

- ⅛ tsp. of cayenne

- ½ tsp. of onion powder

- ½ tsp. black pepper freshly ground

Instructions:

1. Preheat your air fryer to 190°c (375°f).

2. Use a medium-size bowl to mix together onion powder, salt, paprika, cayenne, pepper, flour and garlic powder.

3. In 2 separate small cups, add your panko & eggs.

4. Cover onion rings with flour, then with the eggs, and afterward with the panko.

Working in lots, put your onion rings in one layer inside your air fryer & "fry" for 5 to 7 minutes or till you see golden brown color.

5. Using warm marinara sauce to serve.

170.   2. Air fryer sweet potato chips

Cook time: 15 mins

Serving: 2

Difficulty: easy

Ingredients:

- 1 ½ tsp. of kosher salt

- 1 tsp. of dried thyme

- 1 large yam or sweet potato

- ½ tsp. of pepper

- 1 tbsp. of olive oil

Instructions:

1. Preheat your air fryer to a degree of 350 f (180 c).

2. Slice your sweet potato have a length of 3- to 6-mm (1/8-1/4-inch). In a medium tub, mix your olive oil with slices of sweet potato until well-seasoned. Add some pepper, thyme and salt to cover.

3. Working in groups, add your chips in one sheet & fry for around 14 minutes till you see a golden brown color and slightly crisp.

Fun.

171.   3. Air fryer tortilla chips

Cook time: 5 mins

Serving: 2 people

Difficulty: easy

Ingredients:

- 1 tbsp. of olive oil

- Guacamole for serving

- 2 tsp. of kosher salt

- 12 corn of tortillas

- 1 tbsp. of McCormick delicious jazzy spice blend

Instructions:

1. Preheat your air fryer at a degree of 350 f (180 c).

2. Gently rub your tortillas with olive oil on every side.

3. Sprinkle your tortillas with delicious jazzy spice and salt mix on every side.

Slice every tortilla into six wedges.

4. Functioning in groups, add your tortilla wedges inside your air fryer in one layer & fry it for around 5 minutes or until you see golden brown color and crispy texture.

Serve adding guacamole

172.   4. Air fryer zesty chicken wings

Cook time: 20 mins

Serving: 2 people

Difficulty: easy

Ingredients:

- 1 ½ tsp. of kosher salt

- 1 ½ lb. of patted dry chicken wings (of 680 g)

- 1 tbsp. of the delicious, zesty spice blend

Instructions:

1. Preheat your air fryer at 190°c (375°f).

2. In a tub, get your chicken wings mixed in salt & delicious zesty spice, which must be blend till well-seasoned.

3. Working in lots, add your chicken wings inside the air fryer in one layer & fry it for almost 20 minutes, turning it halfway through.

4. Serve it warm

5. Air fryer sweet potato fries

Cook time: 15 mins

Serving: 2 people

Difficulty: easy

Ingredients:

- 1/4 tsp. of sea salt

- 1 tbsp. of olive oil

- 2 (having 6-oz.) sweet potatoes, cut & peeled into sticks of 1/4-inch

- Cooking spray

- 1/4 tsp. of garlic powder

- 1 tsp. fresh thyme chopped

Instructions:

1. Mix together thyme, garlic powder, olive oil and salt in a bowl. Put sweet potato inside the mixture and mix well to cover.

2. Coat the basket of the air fryer gently with the help of cooking spray. Place your sweet potatoes in one layer inside the basket & cook in groups at a degree of 400 f until soft inside & finely browned from outside for around 14 minutes, rotating the fries halfway through the cooking process.

Cook time: 30 mins

Serving: 12

Difficulty: easy

Ingredients:

• 1/4 cup, adding 2 tbsp. Unsalted butter that's divided into half-cup (around 2 1/8 oz.)

• 3 tbsp. of heavy cream

• Half cup water

• 4 ounces of bitter and sweet finely chopped baking chocolate

• Flour for All-purpose

• 2 tsp. of ground cinnamon

• 2 large eggs

• 1/4 tsp. of kosher salt

• 2 tbsp. of vanilla kefir

• 1/3 cup of granulated sugar

Instruction:

1. Bring salt, water & 1/4 cup butter and boil it in a tiny saucepan with a medium-high flame. Decrease the heat to around medium-low flame; add flour & mix actively with a spoon made up of wood for around 30 seconds.

2. Stir and cook continuously till the dough is smooth. Do this till you see your dough continues to fall away from the sides of the pan & a film appears on the bottom of the pan after 2 to 3 minutes. Move the dough in a medium-sized bowl. Stir continuously for around 1 minute until slightly cooled. Add one egg from time to time while stirring continuously till you see it gets smoother after every addition. Move the mixture in the piping bag, which is fitted with having star tip of medium size. Chill it for around 30 minutes.

3. Pipe 6 (3" long) bits in one-layer inside a basket of the air fryer. Cook at a degree of 380 f for around 10 minutes. Repeat this step for the leftover dough.

4. Stir the sugar & cinnamon together inside a medium-size bowl. Use 2 tablespoons of melted butter to brush the cooked churros. Cover them with the sugar mixture.

5. Put the cream and chocolate in a tiny, microwaveable tub. Microwave with a high temperature for roughly 30 seconds until molten and flat, stirring every 15 seconds. Mix in kefir.

6. Serve the churros, including chocolate sauce.

175.   7. Whole-wheat pizzas in an air fryer

Cook time: 10 mins

Serving: 2 people

Difficulty: easy

Ingredients:

- 1 small thinly sliced garlic clove

- 1/4 ounce of Parmigiano-Reggiano shaved cheese (1 tbsp.)

- 1 cup of small spinach leaves (around 1 oz.)

- 1/4 cup marinara sauce (lower-sodium)

- 1-ounce part-skim pre-shredded mozzarella cheese (1/4 cup)

- 1 tiny plum tomato, sliced into 8 pieces

- 2 pita rounds of whole-wheat

Instructions:

1. Disperse marinara sauce equally on one side of every pita bread. Cover it each with half of the tomato slices, cheese, spinach leaves and garlic.

2. Put 1 pita in the basket of air-fryer & cook it at a degree of 350 f until the cheese is melted and the pita is crispy. Repeat with the leftover pita.

176.   8. Air-fried corn dog bites

Cook time: 15 mins

Serving: 4 people

Difficulty: easy

Ingredients:

- 2 lightly beaten large eggs

- 2 uncured hot dogs of all-beef

- Cooking spray

- 12 bamboo skewers or craft sticks

- 8 tsp. of yellow mustard

- 1 1/2 cups cornflakes cereal finely crushed

- 1/2 cup (2 1/8 oz.) Flour for All-purpose

Instructions:

1. Split lengthwise every hot dog. Cut every half in three same pieces. Add a bamboo skewer or the craft stick inside the end of every hot dog piece.

2. Put flour in a bowl. Put slightly beaten eggs in another shallow bowl. Put crushed cornflakes inside another shallow bowl. Mix the hot dogs with flour; make sure to shake the surplus. Soak in the egg, helping you in dripping off every excess. Dredge inside the cornflakes crumbs, pushing to stick.

3. Gently coat the basket of the air fryer with your cooking spray. Put around six bites of corn dog inside the basket; spray the surface lightly with the help of cooking spray. Now cook at a degree of 375 f till the coating shows a golden brown color and is crunchy for about 10 minutes, flipping the bites of corn dog halfway in cooking. Do this step with other bites of the corn dog.

4. Put three bites of corn dog with 2 tsp. of mustard on each plate to, and then serve immediately.

177.   9. Crispy veggie quesadillas in an air fryer

Cook time: 20 mins

Serving: 4 people

Difficulty: easy

Instructions:

- Cooking spray

- 1/2 cup refrigerated and drained pico de gallo

- 4 ounces far educing cheddar sharp cheese, shredded (1 cup)

- 1 tbsp. of fresh juice (with 1 lime)

- 4(6-in.) whole-grain Sprouted flour tortillas

- 1/4 tsp. ground cumin

- 2 tbsp. fresh cilantro chopped

- 1 cup red bell pepper sliced

- 1 cup of drained & rinsed black beans canned, no-salt-added

- 1 tsp. of lime zest plus

- 1 cup of sliced zucchini

- 2 ounces of plain 2 percent fat reduced Greek yogurt

Instructions:

1. Put tortillas on the surface of your work. Sprinkle two tbsp. Shredded cheese on the half of every tortilla. Each tortilla must be top with cheese, having a cup of 1/4 each black beans, slices of red pepper equally and zucchini slices. Sprinkle equally with the leftover 1/2 cup of cheese. Fold the tortillas making a shape of a half-moon. Coat quesadillas lightly with the help of cooking spray & protect them with toothpicks.

2. Gently spray the cooking spray on the basket of the air fryer. Cautiously put two quesadillas inside the basket & cook it at a degree of 400 f till the tortillas are of golden brown color & slightly crispy, vegetables get softened, and the cheese if

finally melted for around 10 minutes, rotating the quesadillas halfway while cooking. Do this step again with the leftover quesadillas.

3. As the quesadillas are cooking, mix lime zest, cumin, yogurt and lime juice altogether in a small tub. For serving, cut the quesadilla in slices & sprinkle it with cilantro. Serve it with a tablespoon of cumin cream and around 2 tablespoons of pico de gallo.

10. Air-fried curry chickpeas

Cook time: 10 mins

Serving: 4 people

Difficulty: easy

Ingredients:

- 2 tbsp. of curry powder

- Fresh cilantro thinly sliced

- 1(15-oz.) Can chickpeas (like garbanzo beans), rinsed & drained (1 1/2 cups)

- 1/4 tsp. of kosher salt

- 1/2 tbsp. of ground turmeric

- 1/2 tsp. of Aleppo pepper

- 1/4 tsp. of ground coriander

- 2 tbsp. of olive oil

- 1/4 tsp. and 1/8 tsp. of Ground cinnamon

- 2 tbsp. of vinegar (red wine)

- 1/4 tsp. of ground cumin

Instructions:

1. Smash chickpeas softly inside a tub with your hands (don't crush); remove chickpea skins.

2. Apply oil and vinegar to chickpeas, & toss for coating. Add turmeric, cinnamon, cumin, curry powder and coriander; whisk gently so that they can be mixed together.

3. Put chickpeas in one layer inside the bask of air fryer & cook at a degree of 400 f till it's crispy for around 15 mins; shake the chickpeas timely while cooking.

4. Place the chickpeas in a tub. Sprinkle it with cilantro, Aleppo pepper and salt; blend to coat.

179.   11. Air fry shrimp spring rolls with sweet chili sauce.

Cook time: 20 mins

Serving: 4

Difficulty: easy

Ingredients:

• 1 cup of matchstick carrots

• 8 (8" square) wrappers of spring roll

• 2 1/2 tbsp. of divided sesame oil

• 4 ounces of peeled, deveined and chopped raw shrimp

• 1/2 cup of chili sauce (sweet)

• 1 cup of (red) bell pepper julienne-cut

- 2 tsp. of fish sauce

- 3/4 cup snow peas julienne-cut

- 2 cups of cabbage, pre-shredded

- 1/4 tsp. of red pepper, crushed

- 1 tbsp. of lime juice (fresh)

- 1/4 cup of fresh cilantro (chopped)

Instructions:

1. In a large pan, heat around 1 1/2 tsp. of oil until softly smoked. Add carrots, bell pepper and cabbage; Cook, stirring constantly, for 1 to 1 1/2 minutes, until finely wilted. Place it on a baking tray; cool for 5 minutes.

2. In a wide tub, place the mixture of cabbage, snow peas, cilantro, fish sauce, red pepper, shrimp and lime juice; toss to blend.

3. Put the wrappers of spring roll on the surface with a corner that is facing you. Add a filling of 1/4 cup in the middle of every wrapper of spring roll, extending from left-hand side to right in a three-inch wide strip.

4. Fold each wrapper's bottom corner over the filling, stuffing the corner tip under the filling. Fold the corners left & right over the filling. Brush the remaining corner softly with water; roll closely against the remaining corner; press gently to cover. Use 2 teaspoons of the remaining oil to rub the spring rolls.

5. Inside the basket of air fryer, put four spring rolls & cook at a degree of 390 f till it's golden, for 6 - 7 minutes, rotating the spring rolls every 5 minutes. Repeat with the leftover spring rolls. Use chili sauce to serve.

Chapter 5: Dessert recipes

180. 1. Air fryer mores

Cook time: 2 mins

Serving: 2 people

Difficulty: easy

Ingredients:

- 1 big marshmallow

- 2 graham crackers split in half

- 2 square, fine quality chocolate

Instructions:

1. Preheat the air fryer at a degree of 330 f.

2. When preheating, break 2 graham crackers into two to form four squares. Cut 1 big marshmallow into half evenly so that one side can be sticky.

3. Add every half of your marshmallow in a square of one graham cracker & push downwards to stick the marshmallow with graham cracker. You must now have two marshmallows coated with graham crackers & two regular graham crackers.

4. In one layer, put two graham crackers and marshmallows inside your air fryer & cook for about 2 minutes till you can see the marshmallow becoming toasted slightly.

5. Remove immediately and completely and add 1 chocolate square to the toasted marshmallow. Add the rest of the squares of the graham cracker and press down. Enjoy instantly.

181.   2. Easy air fryer brownies

Cook time: 15 mins

Serving: 4 people

Difficulty: easy

Ingredients:

- 2 large eggs

- ½ cup flour for all-purpose

- ¼ cup melted unsalted butter

- 6 tbsp. of cocoa powder, unsweetened

- ¼ tsp. of baking powder

- ¾ cup of sugar

- ½ tsp. of vanilla extract

- 1 tbsp. of vegetable oil

- ¼ tsp. of salt

Instructions:

1. Get the 7-inch baking tray ready by gently greasing it with butter on all the sides and even the bottom. Put it aside

2. Preheat the air fryer by adjusting its temperature to a degree of 330 f & leaving it for around 5 minutes as you cook the brownie batter.

3. Add baking powder, cocoa powder, vanilla extract, flour for all-purpose, butter, vegetable oil, salt, eggs and sugar in a big tub & mix it unless well combined.

4. Add up all these for the preparation of the baking pan & clean the top.

5. Put it inside the air fryer & bake it for about 15 minutes or as long as a toothpick can be entered and comes out easily from the center.

6. Take it out and make it cool in the tray until you remove and cut.

182.   3. Easy air fryer churros

Cook time: 5 mins

Serving: 4 people

Difficulty: easy

Ingredients:

• 1 tbsp. of sugar

- Sifted powdered sugar & cinnamon or cinnamon sugar

- 1 cup (about 250ml) water

- 4 eggs

- ½ cup (113g) butter

- ¼ tsp. salt

- 1 cup (120g) all-purpose flour

Instructions:

1. Mix the ingredients bringing them to boil while stirring continuously.

2. Add flour & start mixing properly. Take it out from the heat & mix it till it gets smooth & the dough can be taken out from the pan easily.

3. Add one egg at one time and stir it until it gets smooth. Set it to cool.

4. Preheat your air fryer degree of 400 for 200 c.

5. Cover your bag of cake decorations with dough & add a star tip of 1/2 inch.

6. Make sticks which are having a length of 3 to 4 inches by moving your dough out from the bag in paper (parchment). You can now switch it inside your air fryer if you are ready to do so. If it is hard to handle the dough, put it inside the refrigerator for around 30 minutes.

7. Use cooking spray or coconut oil to spray the tray or the basket of your air fryer.

8. Add around 8 to 10 churros in a tray or inside the basket of the air fryer. Spray with oil.

9. Cook for 5 minutes at a degree of 400 for 200 c.

10. Until finished and when still hot, rill in regular sugar, cinnamon or sugar mixture.

11. Roll in the cinnamon-sugar blend, cinnamon or normal sugar until finished and when still high.

Cook time: 8 mins

Serving: 4 people

Difficulty: easy

Ingredients:

- ¼ cup of white sugar

- ⅓ Cup of water

- ¼ cup of brown sugar

- ½ tsp. of ground cinnamon

- 6 apples diced and cored

- ¼ tsp. of pumpkin pie spice

- ¼ tsp. of ground cloves

Instructions:

1. Put all the ingredients in a bowl that is oven safe & combine it with water and seasonings. Put the bowl inside the basket, oven tray or even in the toaster of an air fryer.

2. Air fry the mixture of apples at a degree of 350 f for around 6 minutes. Mix the apples & cook them for an extra 2 minutes. Serve it hot and enjoy.

184. 5. Air fryer pear crisp for two

Cook time: 20 mins

Serving: 2

Difficulty: easy

Ingredients:

- ¾ tsp. of divided ground cinnamon

- 1 tbsp. of softened salted butter

- 1 tsp. of lemon juice

- 2 pears. Peeled, diced and cored

- 1 tbsp. of flour for all-purpose

- 2 tbsp. of quick-cooking oats

- 1 tbsp. of brown sugar

Instructions:

1. Your air fryer should be preheated at a degree of 360 f (180 c).

2. Mix lemon juice, 1/4 tsp. Cinnamon and pears in a bowl. Turn for coating and then split the mixture into 2 ramekins.

3. Combine brown sugar, oats, leftover cinnamon and flour in the tub. Using your fork to blend in the melted butter until the mixture is mushy. Sprinkle the pears.

4. Put your ramekins inside the basket of an air fryer & cook till the pears become bubbling and soft for around 18 - 20 minutes.

185.   6. Keto chocolate cake – air fryer recipe

Cook time: 10 mins

Serving: 6 people

Difficulty: easy

Ingredients:

- 1 tsp. of vanilla extract

- 1/2 cup of powdered Swerve

- 1/3 cup of cocoa powder unsweetened

- 1/4 tsp. of salt

- 1 & 1/2 cups of almond flour

- 2 large eggs

- 1/3 cups of almond milk, unsweetened

- 1 tsp. of baking powder

Instructions:

1. In a big mixing tub, mix every ingredient until they all are well mixed.

2. Butter or spray your desired baking dish. We used bunt tins in mini size, but you can even get a 6-inch cake pan in the baskets of the air fryer.

3. Scoop batter equally inside your baking dish or dishes.

4. Set the temperature of the air fryer to a degree of 350 f & set a 10-minute timer. Your cake will be ready when the toothpick you entered comes out clear and clean.

Conclusion:

The air fryer seems to be a wonderful appliance that will assist you with maintaining your diet. You will also enjoy the flavor despite eating high amounts of oil if you prefer deep-fried food.

Using a limited quantity of oil, you will enjoy crunchy & crispy food without the additional adverse risk, which tastes exactly like fried food. Besides, the system is safe & easy to use. All you must do is choose the ingredients needed, and there will be nutritious food available for your family.

An air fryer could be something which must be considered if a person is attempting to eat a diet having a lower-fat diet, access to using the system to prepare a range of foods, & want trouble cooking experience.